Jeremiah Untangled

Jeremiah Untangled

The Book of Jeremiah Arranged Chronologically with Historical Background

edited with commentary by

Charles Siegel

Omo Press

adolescentium alunt
senectutem oblectant

ISBN: 978-1-941667-23-1

This edition uses the Jewish Publication Society translation of 1917. That translation breaks up many verses into poetry with a capital letter at the beginning of each line; this edition combines these verses into continuous paragraphs and drops the unnecessary capitalization. Apart from this, it keeps the punctuation of the JPS translation.

Cover illustration: Horace Vernet, Jeremiah on the Ruins of Jerusalem (1844). Note that Jeremiah had been prophesying for about fifty years at the time of the destruction of Jerusalem, so he was actually much older at the time than he appears to be in this picture.

Contents

Introduction

Jeremiah prophesied for about fifty years, from the thirteenth year of King Josiah (c. 636 BCE) until after the destruction of Jerusalem by the Babylonians (586 BCE).*

It was a tumultuous time politically, and Jeremiah was intensely involved in its politics: he supported the reforms of King Josiah, and he antagonized later kings by condemning them for abandoning these reforms and by telling them that the only way to avoid the destruction of Judah was to accept Babylonian rule. He even wore a yoke to dramatize the idea that Judah should submit to the yoke of Babylonian domination.

It is impossible to understand the prophecies and the stories about him that are collected in the Book of Jeremiah without understanding the political situations that he was responding to. Yet it is difficult to keep the political background each passage in mind, because the Book of Jeremiah is not arranged in chronological order and because many passages quote Jeremiah's prophecies without giving any historical context.

By rearranging the passages that can be dated in chronological order, and by explaining the changing political context of the prophecies, this edition makes it possible for readers who are not experts in ancient history to understand the Book or Jeremiah.

The Texts of the Book of Jeremiah

The Book of Jeremiah is so disorganized because it is a collection of several earlier texts, which are themselves loosely organized

---

* Babylonian records indicate that the Temple was destroyed in 587 BCE. This edition uses the traditional date of 586 BCE, based on Biblical chronology.

collections of shorter documents. The texts that it includes are:

- **The Book of 605 (chapters 1 to 25).** The Book of Jeremiah tells us (36:1-2) that, in the fourth year of king Jehoiakim (605 BCE), Jeremiah was commanded to write down his earlier prophecies. This section of the Book of Jeremiah seems to be based on the text created at that time, but it obviously was expanded later because it has many passages that must have been written after 605. This section is made up of Jeremiah's own statements, with little or no background about his situation when he made these statements.

- **Incidents from Jeremiah's Life (chapters 26 to 28).** This section is a collection of anecdotes about Jeremiah's life.

- **Letter from Jeremiah to the Babylonian Exiles (chapter 29).** Jeremiah wrote this letter to advise Judean exiles in Babylon to be good citizens and be productive economically during what he prophesied would be a long exile.

- **Book of Consolations (chapters 30 to 33).** This text is a collection of miscellaneous prophecies by Jeremiah with the common theme of consolation. There are many disputes among scholars about the dates and authenticity of these statements.

- **Incidents in Jeremiah's Life (chapters 34 to 45).** This is a second collection of anecdotes about Jeremiah's life.

- **Prophecies Against the Nations (chapters 46 to 51).** These verses are in a different location and different order in the Septuagint (the ancient Greek translation of the Bible) than in the Hebrew Bible, indicating that they are a late compilation and addition to the Book of Jeremiah. The earliest prophecies in this section date are probably by Jeremiah, but most were added later, during the Babylonian exile.

- **Historical Epilog (chapter 52).** This section describes the fall of Judah and is similar to 2 Kings 24:15-25:30. It does not mention Jeremiah and is obviously a late addition to the book.

The Book of Jeremiah places these different source texts one after another, with no regard to the underlying history. For example, the text of Jeremiah's Temple Sermon is in Chapter 7 in a collection of the sayings of Jeremiah, while the story of this sermon is in Chapter 26 in a collection of events from Jeremiah's life. In the conventional version of the Book of Jeremiah, readers are unlikely to see the connection between these two passages; in this edition, they are next to each other.

In this edition, the section named "The Historical Narrative" includes all authentic passages that can be dated, arranged in chronological order. The letter to the Babylonian exiles and all the passages in the two collections of incidents in Jeremiah's life are included in this section. About one-third of the passages from the book of 605 can be dated and seem authentic, and they are also included in this section; the rest of the Book of 605 is separate. Only one passage from the Book of Consolations, about Rachel weeping for her children, is probably authentic and is included in this section, while the rest is separate. Two passages from the Book of Prophecies Against the Nations are probably authentic and are included in this section, while the rest is separate. The Historical Epilog is a late addition and is separate.

Removing the late additions and the passages that cannot be dated gives us a very clear historical narrative, making it much easier to understand Jeremiah's career and how it was shaped by the events of the time.

Jeremiah's Times

To understand Jeremiah, you have to understand the history of his times. There is brief overview of the history here and more detailed history in the introductions to the passages.

Centuries before Jeremiah, just after the reign of king Solomon, the united kingdom of the twelve tribes of Israel split in two. The northern kingdom of Israel included ten tribes. The southern kingdom of Judah included two tribes (Judah and Simeon, which had been assimilated into Judah). Jerusalem and the Temple were in the territory of Judah.

In 722 BCE, the northern kingdom of Israel was conquered by Assyria and its people were exiled to that country. Hezekiah, the king of Judah at that time, tried to save his kingdom by instituting a strict religious reform that banned the worship of any gods except the Lord. The Bible tells us that Assyria invaded Judah, conquered cities, and received tribute from Hezekiah (2 Kings 18:13-16), but when the Assyrians besieged Jerusalem, an angel came and slaughtered 185,000 of them while they slept, making the Assyrians abandon the siege (2 Kings 19:35-36). This angel may have been a plague that killed Assyrian soldiers, since another text of the Bible identifies a plague with an angel (1 Chron. 21:14-17).

The next Judean kings, Hezekiah's son Manasseh and grandson Amon, abandoned his reforms. His great-grandson Josiah became king in 649 BCE, at the age of eight. In the eighteenth year of Josiah's reign, a previously unknown book of the Torah was discovered in the Temple while it was being repaired. Most scholars believe that this book is Deuteronomy, which is supposedly Moses' farewell address summarizing the Israelites' obligations under the law. The discovery of this book led Josiah to institute a religious reform and to ban all worship of other gods, as Hezekiah had.

Jeremiah began to prophesy in the thirteenth year of Josiah's reign, condemning the worship of other gods. Josiah's reform, five years later, was an immense triumph for his point of view.

During the early part of Josiah's reign, the power of Assyria was declining, so it seemed plausible that Judah could remain independent though it was located between great powers, Egypt to the southwest and Assyria and the newly rising empire of Babylon to the northeast. Much of Judah's subsequent history reflects the struggle for dominance among these three powers, as Egypt tried to prevent the rise of Babylon while Babylon's power continued to grow, leaving Judah divided between those who wanted to ally with Egypt and those who wanted to submit to Babylon to avoid being destroyed.

In 609, the Egyptian army led by Pharaoh Necho II passed through Judah on its way to help Assyria fight Babylon. Josiah was killed in a battle against the Egyptians. His religious reform did not protect him, and it was abandoned after his death, a tremendous defeat for Jeremiah's point of view.

When Josiah died, his son Jehoahaz became king, but his reign only lasted three months. On their way back from Assyria, the Egyptians killed him and installed his brother Jehoiakim as king.

Jehoiakim was installed as a vassal of Egypt, but he shifted allegiance to Babylon and then back to Egypt, depending on which of the two powers seemed to be winning. When he shifted his allegiance back to Egypt, Babylon invaded Judah and besieged Jerusalem. Jehoiakim died during this siege and his son Jehoiachin became king in 598 BCE.

Jehoiachin lasted only three months before the siege succeeded and Jerusalem fell to the Babylonians, who punished Judah by sending the royal family and many craftsmen and smiths to exile in Babylon,

The Babylonians installed Zedekiah, Johoiachin's younger brother, as their puppet king in 597, but from the beginning of his reign, many Judeans said that Zedekiah should break away from the Babylonians. In 589, Pharaoh Hophra began to reign in Egypt, and Zedekiah took the opportunity to ask the Egyptians for help in freeing Judah from the Babylonians.

The Babylonians responded by attacking Judah and besieging Jerusalem. When Jerusalem fell in 586, Babylon imposed a much more severe punishment than it had after the previous rebellion: it razed Jerusalem, demolished its walls, destroyed the Temple, and sent all of the Judeans except the very poor into exile in Babylon.

Throughout this period, Jeremiah was a member of the Babylonian party. He prophesied, with some inconsistency, that Judah could save itself by submitting to Babylon and that Judah would be destroyed for abandoning Josiah's reforms and worshiping other gods. He was a key figure in the fierce political controversies between the Egyptian and the Babylonian parties

In 539, less than fifty years after the exile began, Persia conquered the Babylonian empire and king Cyrus the Great gave the exiled Judeans permission to return to their homeland. The books of Ezra and Nehemiah tell the story of their gradual return.

Jeremiah's Changing Character

Rearranging the book of Jeremiah in chronological order gives us a clearer view of the prophet's character and career. Jeremiah is famous as a fierce prophet of destruction, but that is only true of the later part of his career.

For almost a third of his career, from his calling in the thirteenth year of King Josiah until Josiah's death in 609, Jeremiah's character was very different. During the early years of his career, Jeremiah called for Judah to repent rather than prophesying its inevitable destruction. Then after Josiah's reform began, Jeremiah had many optimistic years when he prophesied that the ten tribes of Israel, exiled in Assyria, also would repent and return from exile. It was only after the death of Josiah, when later kings abandoned his reforms, that Jeremiah began to make the fierce prophecies of destruction that he is famous for.

The development of Jeremiah's thinking seems very natural. At the beginning of his career, he was hopeful that Judah would repent. During Josiah's reforms, he was optimistic. But when later kings abandoned Josiah's reforms, he became embittered and prophesied that Judah would inevitably be destroyed.

It seems that Jeremiah's behavior also changed after Josiah's death. Before that time, there is no record of any public reaction to his prophecies. After that time, he made his prophecies in public ways that could not be ignored, and the reactions ranged from threatened violence to imprisonment. These high-profile prophecies begin with the Temple Sermon, made in the Temple in Jerusalem at a time when all the Judeans were gathered there (26:2). The reactions to the Temple sermon sound as if the public did not know much about Jeremiah and were just making up their mind about him (26:10-19).

These changes are hard to notice when we read the book of Jeremiah in its conventional form, partly because more of the late prophecies than of the early prophecies survive, and partly because many of the early prophecies are interwoven with later texts and are hard to identify. But when we arrange the book in chronological order, it becomes clear that Jeremiah began as an obscure and sometimes optimistic prophet. It was only after the death of Josiah and abandonment of his reforms that Judah's desperate situation led him to thrust himself into the midst of the public debate and to make the fierce prophecies of destruction that he is famous for, while at the same time being realistic enough to say that Judah could save itself by accepting Babylonian domination.

The books of Jeremiah and of Kings both condemn Judah's disobedience, but there is a significant difference. The book of Kings focuses solely on punishment for worshipping other gods. Jeremiah, in the best prophetic tradition, predicts punishment for moral failings as well as for worshipping other gods.

The Historical Narrative

This section rearranges texts from the two collections of incidents from Jeremiah's life, the letter to the exiles in Babylon, parts of the Book of 605, and a few passages from the Book of Consolations and the Book of Prophecies Against the Nations, placing them in chronological order to form a coherent historical narrative.

Reign of Josiah: c. 649-609 BCE

Josiah became king in about 649, when his father, King Amon, was assassinated. In eighteenth year of his reign, a scroll of the law was discovered during renovation of the Temple, which inspired Josiah to institute a religious reform, banning the worship of other gods. Josiah's purification of the religion roused optimism that God would allow Judah to remain independent.

At this time, Assyria was beginning to lose its power, and the power vacuum made it seem plausible that Judah could escape from the influence of the surrounding empires, but the Babylonians tried to fill this power vacuum and the Egyptians tried to stop them. In 609, Pharaoh Necho II of Egypt led an army to help Assyria against the Babylonians, to prevent Babylon from gaining more power. Josiah's army fought against the Egyptians at Megiddo, and Josiah was killed.

Before Josiah's religious reform of 631, Jeremiah condemned Judah's immorality and worship of pagan gods and called for repentance. After this reform, Jeremiah was optimistic and he even prophesied that the ten tribes of Israel would return from their exile to worship God in Jerusalem.

Prologue (1:1-1:3)

Because scrolls do not have title pages, the Book of Jeremiah begins with this prologue identifying the author.

^{1:1}The words of Jeremiah the son of Hilkiah, of the priests that were in Anathoth in the land of Benjamin, ²to whom the word of the Lord came in the days of Josiah the son of Amon, king of Judah, in the thirteenth year of his reign. ³It came also in the days of Jehoiakim the son of Josiah, king of Judah, unto the end of the eleventh year of Zedekiah the son of Josiah, king of Judah, unto the carrying away of Jerusalem captive in the fifth month.

The Calling of Jeremiah (1:4-1:10)

This passage from the Book of 605 describes how Jeremiah was called to be a prophet.

^{1:4}And the word of the Lord came unto me, saying: ⁵Before I formed thee in the belly I knew thee, and before thou camest forth out of the womb I sanctified thee; I have appointed thee a prophet unto the nations.

⁶Then said I: 'Ah, Lord God! Behold, I cannot speak; for I am a child.'

⁷But the Lord said unto me: Say not: I am a child; for to whomsoever I shall send thee thou shalt go, and whatsoever I shall command thee thou shalt speak. ⁸Be not afraid of them; for I am with thee to deliver thee, saith the Lord.

⁹Then the Lord put forth His hand, and touched my mouth; and the Lord said unto me: Behold, I have put My words in thy mouth; ¹⁰See, I have this day set thee over the nations and over

the kingdoms, to root out and to pull down, and to destroy and to overthrow; to build, and to plant.

Two Early Visions (1:11-1:17)

These two visions from the Book of 605 came near the beginning of Jeremiah's calling, perhaps immediately after the calling or perhaps a bit later. They contain the first statement of one of Jeremiah's central ideas: that an invader will destroy Judah as a punishment for worshipping other gods. At this early date, the invader from the north was presumably Assyria.

There is a pun in verse 1:11-12. Hebrew for "almond tree" is shaked, and Hebrew for "watch over" is shoked.

1:11Moreover the word of the Lord came unto me, saying: 'Jeremiah, what seest thou?' And I said: 'I see a rod of an almond-tree.' 12Then said the Lord unto me: 'Thou hast well seen; for I watch over My word to perform it.'

13And the word of the Lord came unto me the second time, saying: 'What seest thou?' And I said: 'I see a seething pot; and the face thereof is from the north.' 14Then the Lord said unto me: 'Out of the north the evil shall break forth upon all the inhabitants of the land. 15For, lo, I will call all the families of the kingdoms of the north, saith the Lord; and they shall come, and they shall set every one his throne at the entrance of the gates of Jerusalem, and against all the walls thereof round about, and against all the cities of Judah. 16And I will utter My judgments against them touching all their wickedness; in that they have forsaken me, and have offered unto other gods, and worshipped the work of their own hands.

17Thou therefore gird up thy loins, and arise, and speak unto them all that I command thee; be not dismayed at them, lest I dismay thee before them. 18For, behold, I have made thee this day a fortified city, and an iron pillar, and brazen walls, against the whole land, against the kings of Judah, against the princes thereof, against the priests thereof, and against the people of the land. ¹⁹And they shall fight against thee; but they shall not prevail against thee; for I am with thee, saith the Lord, to deliver thee.'

Call for Repentance (2:1-4:4, 4:14, 6:8)

These connected passages from the Book of 605 denounce Judah's and Israel's sins and call for repentance. The northern kingdom of Israel has already been punished by exile in Assyria, and Judah is threatened with punishment. A drought in Judah (3:3) is the beginning of this punishment, and exile could be the ultimate punishment.

We can roughly date this prophecy because it says, "³:⁶And the Lord said unto me in the days of Josiah the king." Because it condemns Judah's worship of other gods, it must come before Josiah's reform.

Because Babylon has not yet become very powerful, Jeremiah thinks of Egypt and Assyria as the great threats: "²:³⁶Thou shalt be ashamed of Egypt also, as thou wast ashamed of Asshur [Assyria]." Noph and Tahpanhes (2:16) are two cities in Egypt. Later in his career, Jeremiah always prophesied that Babylon would be the one dominant power, but he has not realized this yet.

This verse is puzzling: "³:¹⁰and yet for all this her treacherous sister Judah hath not returned unto Me with her whole heart, but feignedly, saith the Lord." What was this feigned repentance? Perhaps there was prayer to God during the drought but not an end to idol worship. We do not know.

Jeremiah begins by condemning the worship of other gods, addressing both Judah and the exiled tribes of Israel. He uses the common metaphor that worshipping other gods is like committing adultery. Jeremiah condemns to the "high places" where Judeans worshipped other gods (3:2), but notice that, in addition to the religious sin of worshiping other gods, he also condemns Judah for its moral sins: "²:³⁴Also in thy skirts is found the blood of the souls of the innocent poor."

²:¹And the word of the Lord came to me, saying: ²Go, and cry in the ears of Jerusalem, saying: Thus saith the Lord: I remember for thee the affection of thy youth, the love of thine espousals; how thou wentest after Me in the wilderness, in a land that was not sown. ³Israel is the Lord's hallowed portion, His first-fruits of the increase; all that devour him shall be held guilty, evil shall come upon them, saith the Lord.

⁴Hear ye the word of the Lord, O house of Jacob, and all the families of the house of Israel;

⁵Thus saith the Lord: What unrighteousness have your fathers found in Me, that they are gone far from Me, and have walked after things of nought, and are become nought?

⁶Neither said they: 'Where is the Lord that brought us up out of the land of Egypt; that led us through the wilderness, through a land of deserts and of pits, through a land of drought and of the shadow of death, through a land that no man passed through, and where no man dwelt?'

⁷And I brought you into a land of fruitful fields, to eat the fruit thereof and the good thereof; but when ye entered, ye defiled My land, and made My heritage an abomination.

⁸The priests said not: 'Where is the Lord?' And they that handle the law knew Me not, and the rulers transgressed against Me; the prophets also prophesied by Baal, and walked after things that do not profit.

⁹Wherefore I will yet plead with you, saith the Lord, and with your children's children will I plead. ¹⁰For pass over to the isles of the Kittites, and see, and send unto Kedar, and consider diligently, and see if there hath been such a thing. ¹¹Hath a nation changed its gods, which yet are no gods?

But My people hath changed its glory for that which doth not profit. ¹²Be astonished, O ye heavens, at this, and be horribly afraid, be ye exceeding amazed, saith the Lord. ¹³For My people have committed two evils: they have forsaken Me, the fountain of living waters, and hewed them out cisterns, broken cisterns, that can hold no water.

¹⁴Is Israel a servant? Is he a home-born slave? Why is he

become a prey? [15]The young lions have roared upon him, and let their voice resound; and they have made his land desolate, His cities are laid waste, without inhabitant. [16]The children also of Noph and Tahpanhes feed upon the crown of thy head.

[17]Is it not this that doth cause it unto thee, that thou hast forsaken the Lord thy God, when He led thee by the way?

[18]And now what hast thou to do in the way to Egypt, to drink the waters of Shihor? Or what hast thou to do in the way to Assyria, to drink the waters of the River?

[19]Thine own wickedness shall correct thee, and thy backslidings shall reprove thee: Know therefore and see that it is an evil and a bitter thing, that thou hast forsaken the Lord thy God, neither is My fear in thee, saith the Lord God of hosts.

[20]For of old time I have broken thy yoke, and burst thy bands, and thou saidst: 'I will not transgress'; upon every high hill and under every leafy tree thou didst recline, playing the harlot. [21]Yet I had planted thee a noble vine, wholly a right seed; how then art thou turned into the degenerate plant of a strange vine unto Me?

[22]For though thou wash thee with nitre, and take thee much soap, yet thine iniquity is marked before Me, saith the Lord God.

[23]How canst thou say: 'I am not defiled, I have not gone after the Baalim'? See thy way in the Valley, know what thou hast done; thou art a swift young camel traversing her ways; [24]a wild ass used to the wilderness, that snuffeth up the wind in her desire; her lust, who can hinder it? All they that seek her will not weary themselves; in her month they shall find her.

[25]Withhold thy foot from being unshod, and thy throat from thirst; but thou saidst: 'There is no hope; no, for I have loved strangers, and after them will I go.'

[26]As the thief is ashamed when he is found, so is the house of Israel ashamed; they, their kings, their princes, and their priests, and their prophets; [27]who say to a stock: 'Thou art my father', and to a stone: 'Thou hast brought us forth', for they have turned their back unto Me, and not their face; but in the time of their trouble they will say: 'Arise, and save us.' [28]But where are thy gods that thou hast made thee? Let them arise, if they can save thee in the

time of thy trouble; for according to the number of thy cities are thy gods, O Judah.

²⁹Wherefore will ye contend with Me? Ye all have transgressed against Me, saith the Lord. ³⁰In vain have I smitten your children—they received no correction; your sword hath devoured your prophets, like a destroying lion.

³¹O generation, see ye the word of the Lord: Have I been a wilderness unto Israel? Or a land of thick darkness? Wherefore say My people: 'We roam at large; we will come no more unto Thee'?

³²Can a maid forget her ornaments, or a bride her attire? Yet My people have forgotten Me days without number.

³³How trimmest thou thy way to seek love! Therefore—even the wicked women hast thou taught thy ways; ³⁴Also in thy skirts is found the blood of the souls of the innocent poor; thou didst not find them breaking in; yet for all these things ³⁵thou saidst: 'I am innocent; surely His anger is turned away from me'—Behold, I will enter into judgment with thee, because thou sayest: 'I have not sinned.'

³⁶How greatly dost thou cheapen thyself to change thy way? Thou shalt be ashamed of Egypt also, as thou wast ashamed of Asshur. ³⁷From him also shalt thou go forth, with thy hands upon thy head; for the Lord hath rejected them in whom thou didst trust, and thou shalt not prosper in them, ^{3:1}saying: if a man put away his wife, and she go from him, and become another man's, may he return unto her again? Will not that land be greatly polluted? But thou hast played the harlot with many lovers; and wouldest thou yet return to Me? saith the Lord.

²Lift up thine eyes unto the high hills, and see: Where hast thou not been lain with? By the ways hast thou sat for them, as an Arabian in the wilderness; and thou hast polluted the land with thy harlotries and with thy wickedness.

³Therefore the showers have been withheld, and there hath been no latter rain; yet thou hadst a harlot's forehead, thou refusedst to be ashamed.

⁴Didst thou not just now cry unto Me: 'My father, Thou art the

friend of my youth. ⁵Will He bear grudge for ever? Will He keep it to the end?' Behold, thou hast spoken, but hast done evil things, and hast had thy way.

Next, Jeremiah addresses the ten tribes of Israel that are exiled in Assyria and says that they can be forgiven even though they have played the harlot with other gods. Because Assyria is north of Judah, he says: "³:¹²Go, and proclaim these words toward the north, and say: Return, thou backsliding Israel."

This seems to be a separate prophecy because it begins with a new introduction ("³:⁶And the Lord said unto me in the days of Josiah the king") and because it is addressed to Israel, but it clearly continues the theme of harlotry from the previous passage. It is probably best to think of these three passages as one connected text, beginning by threatening destruction to Judah and Israel, then calling on Israel to repent and avoid destruction, and then calling on Judah to repent and avoid destruction.

Verses 3:16-18 are a later addition. The ark of the covenant was central to the first Temple, but it was lost when Jerusalem was destroyed. These verses were added after the exile to defend the second Temple, saying it does not need the ark.

³:⁶And the Lord said unto me in the days of Josiah the king: 'Hast thou seen that which backsliding Israel did? She went up upon every high mountain and under every leafy tree, and there played the harlot. ⁷And I said: After she hath done all these things, she will return unto me; but she returned not. And her treacherous sister Judah saw it. ⁸And I saw, when, forasmuch as backsliding Israel had committed adultery, I had put her away and given her a bill of divorcement, that yet treacherous Judah her sister feared not; but she also went and played the harlot; ⁹and it came to pass through the lightness of her harlotry, that the land was polluted, and she committed adultery with stones and with stocks; ¹⁰and yet for all this her treacherous sister Judah hath not returned unto Me with her whole heart, but feignedly, saith the Lord—¹¹even the Lord said unto me—backsliding Israel hath proved herself more righteous than treacherous Judah.

¹²Go, and proclaim these words toward the north, and say: Return, thou backsliding Israel, saith the Lord; I will not frown upon you; for I am merciful, saith the Lord, I will not bear grudge for ever.

¹³Only acknowledge thine iniquity, that thou hast transgressed against the Lord thy God, and hast scattered thy ways to the strangers under every leafy tree, and ye have not hearkened to My voice, saith the Lord.

¹⁴Return, O backsliding children, saith the Lord; for I am a lord unto you, and I will take you one of a city, and two of a family, and I will bring you to Zion; ¹⁵and I will give you shepherds according to My heart, who shall feed you with knowledge and understanding. ¹⁶And it shall come to pass, when ye are multiplied and increased in the land, in those days, saith the Lord, they shall say no more: the ark of the covenant of the Lord; neither shall it come to mind; neither shall they make mention of it; neither shall they miss it; neither shall it be made any more. ¹⁷At that time they shall call Jerusalem the throne of the Lord; and all the nations shall be gathered unto it, to the name of the Lord, to Jerusalem; neither shall they walk any more after the stubbornness of their evil heart. ¹⁸In those days the house of Judah shall walk with the house of Israel, and they shall come together out of the land of the north to the land that I have given for an inheritance unto your fathers.'

¹⁹But I said: 'How would I put thee among the sons, and give thee a pleasant land, the goodliest heritage of the nations!' And I said: 'Thou shalt call Me, my father; and shalt not turn away from following Me.'

²⁰Surely as a wife treacherously departeth from her husband, so have ye dealt treacherously with Me, O house of Israel, saith the Lord.

²¹Hark! Upon the high hills is heard the suppliant weeping of the children of Israel; for that they have perverted their way, they have forgotten the Lord their God. ²²Return, ye backsliding children, I will heal your backslidings.

—'Here we are, we are come unto Thee; for Thou art the Lord our God. [23]Truly vain have proved the hills, the uproar on the mountains; truly in the Lord our God is the salvation of Israel. [24]But the shameful thing hath devoured the labour of our fathers from our youth; their flocks and their herds, their sons and their daughters. [25]Let us lie down in our shame, and let our confusion cover us; for we have sinned against the Lord our God, we and our fathers, from our youth even unto this day; and we have not hearkened to the voice of the Lord our God.'

[4:1]If thou wilt return, O Israel, saith the Lord, yea, return unto Me; and if thou wilt put away thy detestable things out of My sight, and wilt not waver; [2]and wilt swear: 'As the Lord liveth' in truth, in justice, and in righteousness; then shall the nations bless themselves by Him, and in Him shall they glory.

The final brief section calls on Judah to repent and says that repentance can avoid destruction. In the conventional version of the book, this early prophecy is intertwined with a later prophecy of destruction. Verses 4:5-4:13, from the later prophecy, seem to be about one of the Babylonian invasions, when Judah retreated to fortified cities. This passage and verses 4:15-6:7 are much more characteristic of Jeremiah's later period, when he abandoned hope that Judah would repent. By contrast to these verses, inserted by a later editor, 4:14 and 6:8 form an obvious conclusion to the early prophecy, with its call for repentance.

[4:3]For thus saith the Lord to the men of Judah and to Jerusalem: Break up for you a fallow ground, and sow not among thorns. [4]Circumcise yourselves to the Lord, and take away the foreskins of your heart, ye men of Judah and inhabitants of Jerusalem; lest My fury go forth like fire, and burn that none can quench it, because of the evil of your doings.

[14]O Jerusalem, wash thy heart from wickedness, that thou mayest be saved. How long shall thy baleful thoughts lodge within thee? [6:8]Be thou corrected, O Jerusalem, lest My soul be alienated from thee, lest I make thee desolate, a land not inhabited.

Prayer to End Judah's Drought (14:1-9, 19-22)

Chapter 14, later in the Book of 605, is made up of two interwoven texts. In one, Jeremiah prays that Judah should be spared from being destroyed by drought. In the other, God tells Jeremiah that Judah will be destroyed by sword and fire and that praying for them will not help. These two texts are inconsistent and clearly were combined by a later editor.

The parts of chapter 14 about drought are from early in Jeremiah's career, since the drought is also mentioned in this early passage: "³:²... thou hast polluted the land With thy harlotries and with thy wickedness. ³Therefore the showers have been withheld, and there hath been no latter rain."

This prayer to spare Judah is a key example of Jeremiah's attitude before Josiah's reform, when he still had hope that Judah will repent and not be destroyed. It is often overlooked because it is interwoven with a prophecy of destruction from later in Jeremiah's career to form chapter 14. For more information about how these texts were interwoven, see the section about 14:10-22, 15:1-4 in the section named "The Book of 605."

¹⁴:¹The word of the Lord that came to Jeremiah concerning the droughts.

²Judah mourneth, and the gates thereof languish, they bow down in black unto the ground; and the cry of Jerusalem is gone up. ³and their nobles send their lads for water: they come to the pits, and find no water; their vessels return empty; they are ashamed and confounded, and cover their heads.

⁴Because of the ground which is cracked, for there hath been no rain in the land, the plowmen are ashamed, they cover their heads.

⁵Yea, the hind also in the field calveth, and forsaketh her young, because there is no grass, ⁶and the wild asses stand on the high hills, they gasp for air like jackals; their eyes fail, because there is no herbage.

⁷Though our iniquities testify against us, O Lord, work Thou

for Thy name's sake; for our backslidings are many, we have sinned against Thee.

[8]O Thou hope of Israel, the Saviour thereof in time of trouble, why shouldest Thou be as a stranger in the land, and as a wayfaring man that turneth aside to tarry for a night? [9]Why shouldest thou be as a man overcome, as a mighty man that cannot save? Yet Thou, O Lord, art in the midst of us, and Thy name is called upon us; leave us not.

[19]Hast Thou utterly rejected Judah? Hath Thy soul loathed Zion? Why hast Thou smitten us, and there is no healing for us? We looked for peace, but no good came; and for a time of healing, and behold terror!

[20]We acknowledge, O Lord, our wickedness, even the iniquity of our fathers; for we have sinned against Thee. [21]Do not contemn us, for Thy name's sake, do not dishonour the throne of Thy glory; remember, break not Thy covenant with us.

[22]Are there any among the vanities of the nations that can cause rain? Or can the heavens give showers? Art not Thou He, O Lord our God, and do we not wait for Thee? For Thou hast made all these things.

Rachel Weeping for Her Children (31:15-22)

These passages were probably written when Jeremiah was at his most optimistic, after Josiah implemented his religious reforms. They prophesy that Israel will return from exile and are obviously very different from the prophecies of destruction that Jeremiah is famous for.

Rachel's children were Joseph and Benjamin, and Joseph's children were Ephraim and Manasseh, the two most populous and most powerful tribes of Israel. Thus, the phrase Rachel's children refers to the tribes of Israel that are exiled in Assyria, who Jeremiah predicts will return. This prophecy proved to be wrong: the tribes of Israel remained in exile and disappeared from history as they were assimilated into the surrounding peoples.

There is some doubt about the authenticity of this passage. It is from the Book of Consolations, which contains many prophecies that both Israel and Judah will return that were clearly written during the Babylonian exile, after Jeremiah died. But it seems plausible that this is an early passage that was combined with the later passages of the Book of Consolations; this passage is a natural follow-up to the earlier call for Israel to repent and return (3:6-4:2) at a more optimistic time when repentance seemed more likely.

31:15Thus saith the Lord: A voice is heard in Ramah, lamentation, and bitter weeping, Rachel weeping for her children; she refuseth to be comforted for her children, because they are not.

16Thus saith the Lord: Refrain thy voice from weeping, and thine eyes from tears; for thy work shall be rewarded, saith the Lord; and they shall come back from the land of the enemy. 17And there is hope for thy future, saith the Lord; and thy children shall return to their own border.

18I have surely heard Ephraim bemoaning himself: 'Thou hast chastised me, and I was chastised, as a calf untrained; turn Thou me, and I shall be turned, for Thou art the Lord my God. 19Surely after that I was turned, I repented, and after that I was instructed, I smote upon my thigh; I was ashamed, yea, even confounded, because I did bear the reproach of my youth.'

20Is Ephraim a darling son unto Me? Is he a child that is dandled? For as often as I speak of him, I do earnestly remember him still; therefore My heart yearneth for him, I will surely have compassion upon him, saith the Lord.

21Set thee up waymarks, make thee guide-posts; set thy heart toward the highway, even the way by which thou wentest; return, O virgin of Israel, return to these thy cities.

22How long wilt thou turn away coyly, O thou backsliding daughter? For the Lord hath created a new thing in the earth: a woman shall court a man.

Reign of Jehoahaz: 609 BCE

Jehoahaz, the son of Josiah, became king after Josiah was killed by the Egyptian army while Pharaoh Necho was moving northward to counter the rising power of Babylon by helping Assyria. He was chosen as king at the age of 23, even though he was younger than his brother Jehoiakim. But he reigned for only a few months, from Tammuz (July) to Tishri (October) 609 BCE. Then Pharaoh Necho, on his way back to Egypt from the north, took Jehoahaz as a captive and installed Jehoiakim as a vassal king who would be subordinate to Egypt.

Jehoahaz was the throne name he took when he became king. Jeremiah refers to him by his original name, Shallum.

The book of Kings just tells us this about him: "[2 Kings23:31]Jehoahaz was twenty and three years old when he began to reign; and he reigned three months in Jerusalem; and his mother's name was Hamutal the daughter of Jeremiah of Libnah. [32]And he did that which was evil in the sight of the Lord, according to all that his fathers had done. [33]And Pharaoh-necoh put him in bands at Riblah in the land of Hamath, that he might not reign in Jerusalem; and put the land to a fine of a hundred talents of silver, and a talent of gold. [34]And Pharaoh-necoh made Eliakim the son of Josiah king in the room of Josiah his father, and changed his name to Jehoiakim; but he took Jehoahaz away; and he came to Egypt, and died there."

The verse "[2 Kings23:32]And he did that which was evil in the sight of the Lord" is this book's typical way of saying that a king allowed worship of other gods. But if Jehoahaz had really abandoned Josiah's reforms and allowed worship of other gods, why didn't Jeremiah condemn him for it? Most of 2 Kings is meant to show that, if kings worship other gods, they or their descendents will be punished. It is possible that the book of Kings claimed that Jehoahaz abandoned Josiah's reforms to teach its usual lesson: if a king is deposed and exiled after such a short time, it must be a punishment for worshiping other gods. Of course, we can only speculate about whether Jehoahaz continued or abandoned Josiah's reforms, and we do not know.

Weep for Jehoahaz (22:10-22:12)

*This brief passage was obviously written just after the exile of
Jehoahaz in 609, but its content is puzzling. It is hard to guess
Jeremiah's attitude toward Jehoahaz (Shallum) based on a
passage that is so short that it provides little context. It is hard
to understand why Jeremiah says "²²:¹⁰Weep ye not for the dead
[which seems to refer to Josiah], neither bemoan him; but weep
sore for him that goeth away [Jehoahaz]." Why does Jeremiah
want us to weep for Jehoahaz? One plausible explanation is
that Jehoahaz continued Josiah's reforms, despite what the book
of Kings says, and that Jeremiah meant we should weep not for
individual kings but for the end of the reforms—which happened
not when Josiah died but when Jehoahaz was exiled. Again, this is
speculation, and we do not know.*

²²:¹⁰Weep ye not for the dead, neither bemoan him; but weep sore
for him that goeth away, for he shall return no more, nor see his
native country. ¹¹For thus saith the Lord touching Shallum the son
of Josiah, king of Judah, who reigned instead of Josiah his father,
and who went forth out of this place: he shall not return thither any
more; ¹²but in the place whither they have led him captive, there
shall he die, and he shall see this land no more.

Reign of Jehoiakim: 608-598 BCE

Jehoiakim reigned from 608 to 598 BCE, as Egypt and Babylon
struggled for dominance, and he changed his allegiance to
whichever power seemed to be winning.

Egypt made him king after deposing Jehoahaz in 608, and he
ruled as a vassal of Egypt, paying them tribute. However, in 605,
when Babylon defeated Egypt in the battle of Carchemish and
Nebuchadnezzar† II besieged Jerusalem, Jehoiakim began paying

---

† The Bible uses the names "Nebuchadnezzar" and "Nebuchadrezzar." This edition uses the traditional "Nebuchadnezzar."

tribute to Babylon instead and gave it members of the royal family as hostages. Then in 601, when Babylon's invasion of Egypt failed, Jehoiakim changed his allegiance back to Egypt. In 598, the Babylonians punished him for supporting Egypt by besieging Jerusalem again; the siege lasted three months, and Jehoiakim died before it ended.

Jeremiah's character seems to have changed when Jehoiakim became king. The book of Jeremiah includes earlier prophecies from the time of Josiah, but it says nothing about where he made these prophecies or whether they had any public effect. By contrast, after Jehoiakim became king, Jeremiah began to make prophecies in public ways that could not be ignored and that provoked kings to punish him, beginning shortly after Jehoiakim became king by delivering his Temple sermon in the court of the Temple when the Judeans were gathered there.

This was a risky business. As part of the story of the Temple sermon, we learn that Jehoiakim had already executed the prophet Uriah ben Shemiah who criticized him and called for strict religious observance (26:20-23). showing us that Jeremiah was not the first prophet to speak against Jehoiakim. There must have been a delay between Jehoiakim becoming king and Jeremiah going out to denounce him in public, since pursuing and killing Uriah ben Shemiah must have taken some time.

Story of the Temple Sermon (26:1-24)

One of the collections of stories about the events of Jeremiah's life includes this description of how the Temple Sermon occurred. Most people did not seem to be familiar with Jeremiah at the time, arguing about whether he should be put to death or should be respected as a prophet (26:8, 11, 16, 19).

Ahikam ben Shaphan, who finally saved Jeremiah's life after this sermon (26:24) was an early backer of Josiah's reforms. He was one of the five people whom Josiah sent to ask Huldah the prophetess about the scroll that was found in the Temple and who brought back her response encouraging reform (2 Kings 22:12-

20, 2 Chron. 34:19-28). Thus, it is not surprising that Ahikam protected Jeremiah when he denounced Jehoiakim for abandoning Josiah's reforms.

Notice that in this first sermon after the end of reform, Jeremiah still believes the people might repent and save themselves (26:3).

²⁶:¹In the beginning of the reign of Jehoiakim the son of Josiah, king of Judah, came this word from the Lord, saying: ²'Thus saith the Lord: Stand in the court of the Lord's house, and speak unto all the cities of Judah, which come to worship in the Lord's house, all the words that I command thee to speak unto them; diminish not a word. ³It may be they will hearken, and turn every man from his evil way; that I may repent Me of the evil, which I purpose to do unto them because of the evil of their doings. ⁴And thou shalt say unto them: Thus saith the Lord: If ye will not hearken to Me, to walk in My law, which I have set before you, ⁵to hearken to the words of My servants the prophets, whom I send unto you, even sending them betimes and often, but ye have not hearkened; ⁶then will I make this house like Shiloh, and will make this city a curse to all the nations of the earth.'

⁷So the priests and the prophets and all the people heard Jeremiah speaking these words in the house of the Lord. ⁸Now it came to pass, when Jeremiah had made an end of speaking all that the Lord had commanded him to speak unto all the people, that the priests and the prophets and all the people laid hold on him, saying: 'Thou shalt surely die. ⁹Why hast thou prophesied in the name of the Lord, saying: This house shall be like Shiloh, and this city shall be desolate, without an inhabitant?' And all the people were gathered against Jeremiah in the house of the Lord.

¹⁰When the princes of Judah heard these things, they came up from the king's house unto the house of the Lord; and they sat in the entry of the new gate of the Lord's house. ¹¹Then spoke the priests and the prophets unto the princes and to all the people, saying: 'This man is worthy of death; for he hath prophesied against this city, as ye have heard with your ears.'

¹²Then spoke Jeremiah unto all the princes and to all the people, saying: 'The Lord sent me to prophesy against this house

and against this city all the words that ye have heard. [13]Therefore now amend your ways and your doings, and hearken to the voice of the Lord your God; and the Lord will repent Him of the evil that He hath pronounced against you. [14]But as for me, behold, I am in your hand; do with me as is good and right in your eyes. [15]Only know ye for certain that, if ye put me to death, ye will bring innocent blood upon yourselves, and upon this city, and upon the inhabitants thereof; for of a truth the Lord hath sent me unto you to speak all these words in your ears.'

[16]Then said the princes and all the people unto the priests and to the prophets: 'This man is not worthy of death; for he hath spoken to us in the name of the Lord our God.'

[17]Then rose up certain of the elders of the land, and spoke to all the assembly of the people, saying: [18]'Micah the Morashtite prophesied in the days of Hezekiah king of Judah; and he spoke to all the people of Judah, saying: "Thus saith the Lord of hosts: Zion shall be plowed as a field, and Jerusalem shall become heaps, and the mountain of the house as the high places of a forest." [19]Did Hezekiah king of Judah and all Judah put him at all to death? Did he not fear the Lord, and entreat the favour of the Lord, and the Lord repented Him of the evil which He had pronounced against them? Thus might we procure great evil against our own souls.'

[20]And there was also a man that prophesied in the name of the Lord, Uriah the son of Shemaiah of Kiriath-jearim; and he prophesied against this city and against this land according to all the words of Jeremiah; [21]and when Jehoiakim the king, with all his mighty men, and all the princes, heard his words, the king sought to put him to death; but when Uriah heard it, he was afraid, and fled, and went into Egypt; [22]and Jehoiakim the king sent men into Egypt, Elnathan the son of Achbor, and certain men with him, into Egypt; [23]and they fetched forth Uriah out of Egypt, and brought him unto Jehoiakim the king; who slew him with the sword, and cast his dead body into the graves of the children of the people.

[24]Nevertheless the hand of Ahikam the son of Shaphan was with Jeremiah, that they should not give him into the hand of the people to put him to death.

Text of the Temple Sermon (7:1-15, 7:20-26)

The Book of 605, which is a collection of the prophet's sayings, gives the text of the Temple Sermon.

The text from 7:1-15, ending with the threat that Jerusalem will be destroyed like Shiloh if they don't obey, corresponds to the description of the Temple Sermon in 26:4-6. There is a change in 7:16-19: Jeremiah was speaking to the people in the Temple, but at this point, God begins speaking to Jeremiah. Then, in 7:20-26, Jeremiah is speaking to the people again, and in 7:27-8:3, God is speaking to Jeremiah again.

It seems that, two texts have been interwoven here, one of Jeremiah speaking to the people, which we keep here as the Temple sermon, and one of God speaking to Jeremiah, which is moved to the section "The Book of 605." Verses 7:1-15 are clearly the text of the Temple Sermon, since they correspond to the description in 26:4-6. 7:27-8:3 may be part of the Temple Sermon, or may be a later addition.

Notice that, in this key sermon, Jeremiah demands moral behavior as well as exclusive worship of God (7:5-9a).

7:1The word that came to Jeremiah from the Lord, saying: 2Stand in the gate of the Lord's house, and proclaim there this word, and say: Hear the word of the Lord, all ye of Judah, that enter in at these gates to worship the Lord.

3Thus saith the Lord of hosts, the God of Israel: Amend your ways and your doings, and I will cause you to dwell in this place. 4Trust ye not in lying words, saying: 'The temple of the Lord, the temple of the Lord, the temple of the Lord, are these.' 5Nay, but if ye thoroughly amend your ways and your doings; if ye thoroughly execute justice between a man and his neighbour; 6if ye oppress not the stranger, the fatherless, and the widow, and shed not innocent blood in this place, neither walk after other gods to your hurt; 7then will I cause you to dwell in this place, in the land that I gave to your fathers, for ever and ever.

8Behold, ye trust in lying words, that cannot profit. 9Will ye steal, murder, and commit adultery, and swear falsely, and offer unto Baal, and walk after other gods whom ye have not known, [10]and come and stand before Me in this house, whereupon My name is called, and say: 'We are delivered', that ye may do all these abominations? [11]Is this house, whereupon My name is called, become a den of robbers in your eyes?

Behold, I, even I, have seen it, saith the Lord. [12]For go ye now unto My place which was in Shiloh, where I caused My name to dwell at the first, and see what I did to it for the wickedness of My people Israel. [13]And now, because ye have done all these works, saith the Lord, and I spoke unto you, speaking betimes and often, but ye heard not, and I called you, but ye answered not; [14]therefore will I do unto the house, whereupon My name is called, wherein ye trust, and unto the place which I gave to you and to your fathers, as I have done to Shiloh. [15]And I will cast you out of My sight, as I have cast out all your brethren, even the whole seed of Ephraim.

[20]Therefore thus saith the Lord God: Behold, Mine anger and My fury shall be poured out upon this place, upon man, and upon beast, and upon the trees of the field, and upon the fruit of the land; and it shall burn, and shall not be quenched.

[21]Thus saith the Lord of hosts, the God of Israel: Add your burnt-offerings unto your sacrifices, and eat ye flesh. [22]For I spoke not unto your fathers, nor commanded them in the day that I brought them out of the land of Egypt, concerning burnt-offerings or sacrifices; [23]but this thing I commanded them, saying: 'Hearken unto My voice, and I will be your God, and ye shall be My people; and walk ye in all the way that I command you, that it may be well with you.' [24]But they hearkened not, nor inclined their ear, but walked in their own counsels, even in the stubbornness of their evil heart, and went backward and not forward, [25]even since the day that your fathers came forth out of the land of Egypt unto this day; and though I have sent unto you all My servants the prophets, sending them daily betimes and often, [26]yet they hearkened not unto Me, nor inclined their ear, but made their neck stiff; they did worse than their fathers.

In Topheth and Jerusalem (19:1 - 20:6)

Later in the book of 605, there is an account of sermons that Jeremiah delivered in Topheth and then in the Temple in Jerusalem. Because the book of 605 is primarily a collection of Jeremiah's sayings, there is little narrative framing this account, and we do not know exactly when these sermons happened.

We can roughly date this passage. It seems that Jeremiah stopped entering the Temple some time before 605, because when he wrote the scroll of 605, he told Baruch "36:5'I am detained, I cannot go into the house of the Lord; 6therefore go thou, and read in the roll, which thou hast written from my mouth." Thus, we can guess that this second sermon in the Temple was early in Jehoiakim's reign, while Jeremiah was still going into the Temple.

At this point, Jeremiah realized that Babylon was the greatest threat to Judah, saying "19:5Moreover I will give all the store of this city ... into the hand of their enemies, who shall spoil them, and take them, and carry them to Babylon." He will continue to believe this for the rest of his career, as kings vacillate between Egypt and Babylon.

It seems that Jeremiah was not punished after the Temple sermon, but after this second sermon in the Temple, he was struck by Pashhur ben Immer and given the relatively mild punishment of one day in the stocks. After being let out of the stocks, he continued to prophesy destruction and antagonized the son of the priest who put him in the stocks, saying (among other things) that he will be named Magormissabib, which means "Terror on every side." Then, some time before 605, he stopped going into the Temple, either because he was not allowed to enter or because he feared even worse punishment, so he had to send Baruch there to deliver his message.

The passage begins with a prophecy in Topheth, where the book of Kings tells us that, until Josiah's reform, priests had sacrificed children to the pagan god Moloch (2 Kings 23:10). Baal was often used as a general name for all pagan gods, as it is used here to include Moloch. Based on this passage, it seems that human sacrifice of children was revived after Josiah's death.

19:1Thus said the Lord: Go, and get a potter's earthen bottle, and take of the elders of the people, and of the elders of the priests; 2and go forth unto the valley of the son of Hinnom, which is by the entry of the gate Harsith, and proclaim there the words that I shall tell thee; 3and say: Hear ye the word of the Lord, O kings of Judah, and inhabitants of Jerusalem; thus saith the Lord of hosts, the God of Israel:

Behold, I will bring evil upon this place, which whosoever heareth, his ears shall tingle; 4because they have forsaken Me, and have estranged this place, and have offered in it unto other gods, whom neither they nor their fathers have known, nor the kings of Judah; and have filled this place with the blood of innocents; 5and have built the high places of Baal, to burn their sons in the fire for burnt-offerings unto Baal; which I commanded not, nor spoke it, neither came it into My mind.

6Therefore, behold, the days come, saith the Lord, that this place shall no more be called Topheth, nor The valley of the son of Hinnom, but The valley of slaughter; 7and I will make void the counsel of Judah and Jerusalem in this place; and I will cause them to fall by the sword before their enemies, and by the hand of them that seek their life; and their carcasses will I give to be food for the fowls of the heaven, and for the beasts of the earth; 8and I will make this city an astonishment, and a hissing; every one that passeth thereby shall be astonished and hiss because of all the plagues thereof; 9and I will cause them to eat the flesh of their sons and the flesh of their daughters, and they shall eat every one the flesh of his friend, in the siege and in the straitness, wherewith their enemies, and they that seek their life, shall straiten them.

10Then shalt thou break the bottle in the sight of the men that go with thee, 11and shalt say unto them: Thus saith the Lord of hosts: Even so will I break this people and this city, as one breaketh a potter's vessel, that cannot be made whole again; and they shall bury in Topheth, for want of room to bury. 12Thus will I do unto this place, saith the Lord, and to the inhabitants thereof, even making this city as Topheth; 13and the houses of Jerusalem, and the houses of the kings of Judah, which are defiled, shall be as the place of Topheth, even all the houses upon whose roofs they have offered unto all the host of heaven, and have poured out drink-offerings unto other gods.

[14]Then came Jeremiah from Topheth, whither the Lord had sent him to prophesy; and he stood in the court of the Lord's house, and said to all the people: [15]'Thus saith the Lord of hosts, the God of Israel: Behold, I will bring upon this city and upon all her towns all the evil that I have pronounced against it; because they have made their neck stiff, that they might not hear My words.'

[20:1]Now Pashhur the son of Immer the priest, who was chief officer in the house of the Lord, heard Jeremiah prophesying these things. [2]Then Pashhur smote Jeremiah the prophet, and put him in the stocks that were in the upper gate of Benjamin, which was in the house of the Lord. [3]And it came to pass on the morrow, that Pashhur brought forth Jeremiah out of the stocks.

Then said Jeremiah unto him: 'The Lord hath not called thy name Pashhur, but Magormissabib. [4]For thus saith the Lord: Behold, I will make thee a terror to thyself, and to all thy friends; and they shall fall by the sword of their enemies, and thine eyes shall behold it; and I will give all Judah into the hand of the king of Babylon, and he shall carry them captive to Babylon, and shall slay them with the sword. [5]Moreover I will give all the store of this city, and all the gains thereof, and all the wealth thereof, yea, all the treasures of the kings of Judah will I give into the hand of their enemies, who shall spoil them, and take them, and carry them to Babylon. [6]And thou, Pashhur, and all that dwell in thy house shall go into captivity; and thou shalt come to Babylon, and there thou shalt die, and there shalt thou be buried, thou, and all thy friends, to whom thou hast prophesied falsely.'

Condemning Jehoiakim's Palace (22:13 -19)

Based on this passage, Jehoiakim apparently conscripted labor to build himself a palace. Jeremiah predicts that he will suffer for this injustice and compares him with his righteous father, Josiah. Notice that Jeremiah condemns Jehoiakim for his immoral behavior and admires Josiah for his moral righteousness and does not even mention Josiah's religious reform or Jehoiakim's Baal worship.

There is no other account of Jehoiakim's building a palace, so it is difficult to date this passage precisely within his reign. Some scholars claim that this passage must be from the early reign of Jehoiakim because Jeremiah dropped out of public life temporarily after writing the book of 605, but we do not know with certainty if this is true. Jeremiah did preach to the Rechabites late in Jehoiakim's reign, and there are many undateable prophecies of destruction that could also have come during Jehoiakim's reign. The best we can do it to say that this passage comes during Jehoiakim's reign.

22:13Woe unto him that buildeth his house by unrighteousness, and his chambers by injustice; that useth his neighbour's service without wages, and giveth him not his hire; 14that saith: 'I will build me a wide house and spacious chambers', and cutteth him out windows, and it is ceiled with cedar, and painted with vermilion.

15Shalt thou reign, because thou strivest to excel in cedar? Did not thy father eat and drink, and do justice and righteousness? Then it was well with him. 16He judged the cause of the poor and needy; then it was well. Is not this to know Me? saith the Lord.

17But thine eyes and thy heart are not but for thy covetousness, and for shedding innocent blood, and for oppression, and for violence, to do it.

18Therefore thus saith the Lord concerning Jehoiakim the son of Josiah, king of Judah: They shall not lament for him: 'Ah my brother!' or: 'Ah sister!' They shall not lament for him: 'Ah lord!' or: 'Ah his glory!' 19He shall be buried with the burial of an ass, drawn and cast forth beyond the gates of Jerusalem.

Concluding the Book of 605 (25:1 - 14)

This passage dates itself by saying it is in the fourth year of Jehoiakim, 605, which is the year that Nebuchadnezzar became king of Babylon—and is also the year that Jeremiah began to write down his earlier prophecies in the Book of 605. This passage begins with a retrospective look at his career (25:3-10), which is appropriate as he begins to write down his earlier prophecies. (25:11-36 is a later addition, so it is in the section "The Book of 605.")

There are indications that this is the time when Jeremiah gave up hope that Judah would repent and began to prophesy that it would inevitably be destroyed. When he is first commanded to write the book, God says, "36:3It may be that the house of Judah will hear all the evil which I purpose to do unto them; that they may return every man from his evil way, and I may forgive their iniquity and their sin," so it is still possible for Judah to save itself, and as they begin to write, he says he has hope of repentance (36:7) But as he looks back at his earlier career, Jeremiah seems to give up all hope that Judah would repent (25:4-11a), and the reception of the book (36:20-26) was not encouraging. After this time, his prophecies emphasize destruction rather than repentance—though, with some inconsistency, he still works hard to convince Judah that it can survive by submitting to the Babylonians

Verse 25:11b prophesies an exile of seventy years, as does Jeremiah's letter to the exiles in Babylon. If this passage is actually a retrospective written at the same time as the book of 605, the prophecy of a seventy-year exile is probably a later addition, written after the exile that followed Jehoiachin's reign. Therefore, this edition includes 25:11a as part of this retrospective and 25:11b as the beginning of a later exilic addition to this retrospective (25:11b-38), which is in the section titled "The Book of 605.". For more information about the seventy-year exile, see the commentary on the letter to the exiles in Babylon (29:1-32).

Jeremiah continues to predict that Babylon will dominate the entire region, as he did during the rest of his career.

25:1The word that came to Jeremiah concerning all the people of Judah in the fourth year of Jehoiakim the son of Josiah, king of Judah, that was the first year of Nebuchadrezzar king of Babylon; 2which Jeremiah the prophet spoke unto all the people of Judah, and to all the inhabitants of Jerusalem, saying:

3From the thirteenth year of Josiah the son of Amon, king

of Judah, even unto this day, these three and twenty years, the word of the Lord hath come unto me, and I have spoken unto you, speaking betimes and often; but ye have not hearkened. ⁴And the Lord hath sent unto you all His servants the prophets, sending them betimes and often—but ye have not hearkened, nor inclined your ear to hear—⁵saying: 'Return ye now every one from his evil way, and from the evil of your doings, and dwell in the land that the Lord hath given unto you and to your fathers, for ever and ever; ⁶and go not after other gods to serve them, and to worship them, and provoke Me not with the work of your hands, and I will do you no hurt.'

⁷Yet ye have not hearkened unto Me, saith the Lord; that ye might provoke Me with the work of your hands to your own hurt. ⁸Therefore thus saith the Lord of hosts: Because ye have not heard My words, ⁹behold, I will send and take all the families of the north, saith the Lord, and I will send unto Nebuchadrezzar the king of Babylon, My servant, and will bring them against this land, and against the inhabitants thereof, and against all these nations round about; and I will utterly destroy them, and make them an astonishment, and a hissing, and perpetual desolations. ¹⁰Moreover I will cause to cease from among them the voice of mirth and the voice of gladness, the voice of the bridegroom and the voice of the bride, the sound of the millstones, and the light of the lamp. ¹¹ᵃAnd this whole land shall be a desolation, and a waste ....

Writing the Book of 605 (36:1-32)

These passages, from one of the collections of stories about Jeremiah's life, tell us how the Book of 605 was written. In the fourth year of Jehoiakim's reign (605), Jeremiah told his scribe Baruch to write down all his earlier prophecies and to go and read them in the Temple (36:1), and Baruch went and read them in the ninth month of the fifth year of Jehoiakim's reign (36:9); presumably there was a delay because it took time to write them all down. After the king burned this roll and Jeremiah and Baruch fled to avoid punishment, they rewrote the book with additions (36:32). This is the text that is incorporated, with later additions and changes, as chapters 1 to 25 of the Bible's book of Jeremiah.

The meaning of "36:5I am detained, I cannot go into the house of the Lord" is uncertain. Many scholars believe that the priests banned him from the Temple because of his earlier preaching there, assuming the word "detained" means "banned." However, it is also possible that he means that it would be unwise or risky for him to go to the Temple after being put in the stocks during his last sermon there, with the word "detained" meaning "constrained." Whatever Jeremiah's reason, poor Baruch is now the one who has to take the risk of reading these prophecies in the Temple.

Notice that some members of the court protected Jeremiah and Baruch from the king by advising them to hide, and some asked the king not to burn the book.

36:1 And it came to pass in the fourth year of Jehoiakim the son of Josiah, king of Judah, that this word came unto Jeremiah from the Lord, saying: 2'Take thee a roll of a book, and write therein all the words that I have spoken unto thee against Israel, and against Judah, and against all the nations, from the day I spoke unto thee, from the days of Josiah, even unto this day. 3It may be that the house of Judah will hear all the evil which I purpose to do unto them; that they may return every man from his evil way, and I may forgive their iniquity and their sin.'

4Then Jeremiah called Baruch the son of Neriah; and Baruch wrote from the mouth of Jeremiah all the words of the Lord, which He had spoken unto him, upon a roll of a book. 5And Jeremiah commanded Baruch, saying: 'I am detained, I cannot go into the house of the Lord; 6therefore go thou, and read in the roll, which thou hast written from my mouth, the words of the Lord in the ears of the people in the Lord's house upon a fast-day; and also thou shalt read them in the ears of all Judah that come out of their cities. 7It may be they will present their supplication before the Lord, and will return every one from his evil way; for great is the anger and the fury that the Lord hath pronounced against this people.' 8And

Baruch the son of Neriah did according to all that Jeremiah the prophet commanded him, reading in the book the words of the Lord in the Lord's house.

[9]Now it came to pass in the fifth year of Jehoiakim the son of Josiah, king of Judah, in the ninth month, that they proclaimed a fast before the Lord, all the people in Jerusalem, and all the people that came from the cities of Judah unto Jerusalem. [10]Then did Baruch read in the book the words of Jeremiah in the house of the Lord, in the chamber of Gemariah the son of Shaphan the scribe, in the upper court, at the entry of the new gate of the Lord's house, in the ears of all the people.

[11]And when Micaiah the son of Gemariah, the son of Shaphan, had heard out of the book all the words of the Lord, [12]he went down into the king's house, into the scribe's chamber; and, lo, all the princes sat there, even Elishama the scribe, and Delaiah the son of Shemaiah, and Elnathan the son of Achbor, and Gemariah the son of Shaphan, and Zedekiah the son of Hananiah, and all the princes. [13]Then Micaiah declared unto them all the words that he had heard, when Baruch read the book in the ears of the people.

[14]Therefore all the princes sent Jehudi the son of Nethaniah, the son of Shelemiah, the son of Cushi, unto Baruch, saying: 'Take in thy hand the roll wherein thou hast read in the ears of the people, and come.' So Baruch the son of Neriah took the roll in his hand, and came unto them. [15]And they said unto him: 'Sit down now, and read it in our ears.' So Baruch read it in their ears. [16]Now it came to pass, when they had heard all the words, they turned in fear one toward another, and said unto Baruch: 'We will surely tell the king of all these words.' [17]And they asked Baruch, saying: 'Tell us now: How didst thou write all these words at his mouth?' [18]Then Baruch answered them: 'He pronounced all these words unto me with his mouth, and I wrote them with ink in the book.' [19]Then said the princes unto Baruch: 'Go, hide thee, thou and Jeremiah, and let no man know where ye are.'

[20]And they went in to the king into the court; but they had deposited the roll in the chamber of Elishama the scribe; and they told all the words in the ears of the king. [21]So the king sent Jehudi

to fetch the roll; and he took it out of the chamber of Elishama the scribe. And Jehudi read it in the ears of the king, and in the ears of all the princes that stood beside the king. [22]Now the king was sitting in the winter-house in the ninth month; and the brazier was burning before him. [23]And it came to pass, when Jehudi had read three or four columns, that he cut it with the penknife, and cast it into the fire that was in the brazier, until all the roll was consumed in the fire that was in the brazier.

[24]Yet they were not afraid, nor rent their garments, neither the king, nor any of his servants that heard all these words. [25]Moreover Elnathan and Delaiah and Gemariah had entreated the king not to burn the roll; but he would not hear them. [26]And the king commanded Jerahmeel the king's son, and Seraiah the son of Azriel, and Shelemiah the son of Abdeel, to take Baruch the scribe and Jeremiah the prophet; but the Lord hid them.

[27]Then the word of the Lord came to Jeremiah, after that the king had burned the roll, and the words which Baruch wrote at the mouth of Jeremiah, saying: [28]'Take thee again another roll, and write in it all the former words that were in the first roll, which Jehoiakim the king of Judah hath burned. [29]And concerning Jehoiakim king of Judah thou shalt say: Thus saith the Lord: Thou hast burned this roll, saying: Why hast thou written therein, saying: The king of Babylon shall certainly come and destroy this land, and shall cause to cease from thence man and beast? [30]Therefore thus saith the Lord concerning Jehoiakim king of Judah: He shall have none to sit upon the throne of David; and his dead body shall be cast out in the day to the heat, and in the night to the frost. [31]And I will visit upon him and his seed and his servants their iniquity; and I will bring upon them, and upon the inhabitants of Jerusalem, and upon the men of Judah, all the evil that I have pronounced against them, but they hearkened not.'

[32]Then took Jeremiah another roll, and gave it to Baruch the scribe, the son of Neriah; who wrote therein from the mouth of Jeremiah all the words of the book which Jehoiakim king of Judah had burned in the fire; and there were added besides unto them many like words.

Prophecy About Baruch (45:1-5)

*This passage is a prophecy about Baruch that Jeremiah supposedly
made as he was working with Baruch on writing the book of 605.
Baruch complained (45:3) either about the work of writing or
(more plausibly) about his very dangerous job of being sent to
read the book in the Temple, and Jeremiah prophesied that Baruch
will barely escape with his life when the Babylonians invade.
Jeremiah was obviously a hard person to work for, but Baruch
was still with him in the days of Zedekiah (32:12) and after the
destruction of Jerusalem (43:3,5).*

*The word "prey" is not a good translation in "⁴⁵:⁵I will bring
evil upon all flesh, saith the Lord; but thy life will I give unto thee
for a prey in all places whither thou goest." The Hebrew shalal
is better translated as "booty." Soldiers hope to bring valuable
booty back from war, but when war comes to Baruch, God will
give him only his own life as booty. That is, Baruch will escape
with nothing but his life.*

*This passage comes at the end of the collection of incidents
in Jeremiah's life that is in chapters 34 to 45, following the story
of Jeremiah and Baruch being taken to Egypt after Jerusalem
is destroyed. The text says the prophecy was made much earlier
(45:1); it was probably placed in this location because the
flight to Egypt confirmed this prophecy by showing that Baruch
escaped with his life and nothing else. The odd location raises
the possibility that it was written later and attributed to Jeremiah
after Baruch escaped with only his life.*

⁴⁵:¹The word that Jeremiah the prophet spoke unto Baruch the son
of Neriah, when he wrote these words in a book at the mouth of
Jeremiah, in the fourth year of Jehoiakim the son of Josiah, king
of Judah, saying:

²'Thus saith the Lord, the God of Israel, concerning thee, O
Baruch: Thou didst say: ³Woe is me now! For the Lord hath added
sorrow to my pain; I am weary with my groaning, and I find no
rest.

⁴Thus shalt thou say unto him: Thus saith the Lord: Behold, that which I have built will I break down, and that which I have planted I will pluck up; and this in the whole land. ⁵And seekest thou great things for thyself? Seek them not; for, behold, I will bring evil upon all flesh, saith the Lord; but thy life will I give unto thee for a prey in all places whither thou goest.'

Defeat and Invasion of Egypt (46:2-24)

These two prophecies against Egypt are the only passages in the Book of Prophecies Against the Nations that seem authentic, since they support Jeremiah's work to convince Judah to submit to Babylon rather than allying with Egypt.

The first is about Babylon's defeat of Egypt in the Battle of Carchemish in about 605. After this battle, Jehoiakim abandoned his loyalty to Egypt, which has initially put him in power, and began paying tribute to Babylon. The prophecy clearly supports Jeremiah's efforts to promote submission to Babylon.

The second predicts that Babylon will invade Egypt. In reality, Babylon's invasion of Egypt failed in 601. Presumably, Jeremiah made the second prophecy before Babylon's failed invasion, as part of his effort to make Judah submit to Babylon. After the invasion failed, Jehoiakim abandoned Babylon and renewed to his alliance with Egypt, causing Nebuchadnezzar to invade Judah and besiege Jerusalem.

Jeremiah also predicted a Babylonian invasion of Egypt when he was taken there after the fall of Jerusalem (43:8-13).

⁴⁶:²Of Egypt: concerning the army of Pharaoh-neco king of Egypt, which was by the river Euphrates in Carchemish, which Nebuchadrezzar king of Babylon smote in the fourth year of Jehoiakim the son of Josiah, king of Judah.

³Make ready buckler and shield, and draw near to battle. ⁴Harness the horses, and mount, ye horsemen, and stand forth with your helmets; furbish the spears, put on the coats of mail.

⁵Wherefore do I see them dismayed and turned backward? And

their mighty ones are beaten down, and they are fled apace, and look not back; terror is on every side, saith the Lord. [6]The swift cannot flee away, nor the mighty man escape; in the north by the river Euphrates have they stumbled and fallen.

[7]Who is this like the Nile that riseth up, like the rivers whose waters toss themselves? [8]Egypt is like the Nile that riseth up, and like the rivers whose waters toss themselves; and he saith: 'I will rise up, I will cover the earth, I will destroy the city and the inhabitants thereof.'

[9]Prance, ye horses, and rush madly, ye chariots; and let the mighty men go forth: Cush and Put, that handle the shield, and the Ludim, that handle and bend the bow. [10]for the Lord God of hosts shall have on that day a day of vengeance, that He may avenge Him of His adversaries; and the sword shall devour and be satiate, And shall be made drunk with their blood; for the Lord God of hosts hath a sacrifice in the north country by the river Euphrates.

[11]Go up into Gilead, and take balm, O virgin daughter of Egypt; in vain dost thou use many medicines; there is no cure for thee. [12]The nations have heard of thy shame, and the earth is full of thy cry; for the mighty man hath stumbled against the mighty, they are fallen both of them together.

[46:13]The word that the Lord spoke to Jeremiah the prophet, how that Nebuchadrezzar king of Babylon should come and smite the land of Egypt.

[14]Declare ye in Egypt, and announce in Migdol, and announce in Noph and in Tahpanhes; say ye: 'Stand forth, and prepare thee, for the sword hath devoured round about thee.'

[15]Why is thy strong one overthrown? He stood not, because the Lord did thrust him down. [16]He made many to stumble; yea, they fell one upon another, and said: 'Arise, and let us return to our own people, and to the land of our birth, from the oppressing sword.' [17]They cried there: 'Pharaoh king of Egypt is but a noise; he hath let the appointed time pass by.'

[18]As I live, saith the King, Whose name is the Lord of hosts, surely like Tabor among the mountains, and like Carmel by the sea, so shall he come.

¹⁹O thou daughter that dwellest in Egypt, furnish thyself to go into captivity; for Noph shall become a desolation, and shall be laid waste, without inhabitant.

²⁰Egypt is a very fair heifer; but the gadfly out of the north is come, it is come. ²¹Also her mercenaries in the midst of her are like calves of the stall, for they also are turned back, they are fled away together, they did not stand; for the day of their calamity is come upon them, the time of their visitation.

²²The sound thereof shall go like the serpent's; for they march with an army, and come against her with axes, as hewers of wood. ²³They cut down her forest, saith the Lord, though it cannot be searched; because they are more than the locusts, and are innumerable.

²⁴The daughter of Egypt is put to shame; she is delivered into the hand of the people of the north.

In the House of the Rechabites (35:1-19)

This passage seems to date from this time near the end of Jehoiakim's reign, when Nebuchadnezzar was devastating Judah and the Judeans were retreating to the walled city of Jerusalem, as it says, "³⁵:¹¹But it came to pass, when Nebuchadrezzar king of Babylon came up against the land, that we said: Come, and let us go to Jerusalem for fear of the army of the Chaldeans, and for fear of the army of the Arameans; so we dwell at Jerusalem."

The clan of Rechabites believed they were commanded by their ancestor Jonadab to dwell in tents as nomadic herders. Though the invasion forced them to flee to Jerusalem rather than being nomads, they earned Jeremiah's admiration by continuing to obey their ancestor's command against drinking wine.

³⁵:¹The word which came unto Jeremiah from the Lord in the days of Jehoiakim the son of Josiah, king of Judah, saying: ²'Go unto the house of the Rechabites, and speak unto them, and bring them into the house of the Lord, into one of the chambers, and give them wine to drink.'

³Then I took Jaazaniah the son of Jeremiah, the son of Habazziniah, and his brethren, and all his sons, and the whole house of the Rechabites; ⁴and I brought them into the house of the Lord, into the chamber of the sons of Hanan the son of Igdaliah, the man of God, which was by the chamber of the princes, which was above the chamber of Maaseiah the son of Shallum, the keeper of the door; ⁵and I set before the sons of the house of the Rechabites goblets full of wine, and cups, and I said unto them: 'Drink ye wine.'

⁶But they said: 'We will drink no wine; for Jonadab the son of Rechab our father commanded us, saying: Ye shall drink no wine, neither ye, nor your sons, for ever; ⁷neither shall ye build house, nor sow seed, nor plant vineyard, nor have any; but all your days ye shall dwell in tents, that ye may live many days in the land wherein ye sojourn. ⁸And we have hearkened to the voice of Jonadab the son of Rechab our father in all that he charged us, to drink no wine all our days, we, our wives, our sons, nor our daughters; ⁹nor to build houses for us to dwell in, neither to have vineyard, or field, or seed; ¹⁰but we have dwelt in tents, and have hearkened, and done according to all that Jonadab our father commanded us. ¹¹But it came to pass, when Nebuchadrezzar king of Babylon came up against the land, that we said: Come, and let us go to Jerusalem for fear of the army of the Chaldeans, and for fear of the army of the Arameans; so we dwell at Jerusalem.'

¹²Then came the word of the Lord unto Jeremiah, saying: ¹³'Thus saith the Lord of hosts, the God of Israel: Go, and say to the men of Judah and the inhabitants of Jerusalem: Will ye not receive instruction to hearken to My words? saith the Lord. ¹⁴The words of Jonadab the son of Rechab, that he commanded his sons, not to drink wine, are performed, and unto this day they drink none, for they hearken to their father's commandment; but I have spoken unto you, speaking betimes and often, and ye have not hearkened unto Me. ¹⁵I have sent also unto you all My servants the prophets, sending them betimes and often, saying: Return ye now every man from his evil way, and amend your

doings, and go not after other gods to serve them, and ye shall dwell in the land which I have given to you and to your fathers; but ye have not inclined your ear, nor hearkened unto Me. ¹⁶Because the sons of Jonadab the son of Rechab have performed the commandment of their father which he commanded them, but this people hath not hearkened unto Me; ¹⁷therefore thus saith the Lord, the God of hosts, the God of Israel: Behold, I will bring upon Judah and upon all the inhabitants of Jerusalem all the evil that I have pronounced against them; because I have spoken unto them, but they have not heard, and I have called unto them, but they have not answered.'

¹⁸And unto the house of the Rechabites Jeremiah said: Thus saith the Lord of hosts, the God of Israel: Because ye have hearkened to the commandment of Jonadab your father, and kept all his precepts, and done according unto all that he commanded you; ¹⁹therefore thus saith the Lord of hosts, the God of Israel: There shall not be cut off unto Jonadab the son of Rechab a man to stand before Me for ever.'

Reign of Jehoiachin: 598-597 BCE

Jehoiakim died during the Babylonian siege of Jerusalem. His son Jeconiah replaced him and took the throne name of Jehoiachin, but he reigned only three months and ten days (beginning December 9, 598) before the Babylonian siege succeeded and Jerusalem fell.

The Babylonians punished Judah's for its rebellion by exiling Jehoiachin, much of the royal family, and many of Judah's craftsmen and smiths to Babylon; presumably, they removed the smiths to reduce Judah's capacity to make weapons. They installed Jehoiakim's younger brother Zedekiah as the new king.

Jeremiah wrote these brief passages around the time of the defeat of Jehoiakim, calling him by his original name, Jeconiah, which Jeremiah shortens to Coniah, rather than using the throne name Jehoiakim. These passages are part of the Book of 605, since they are in chapter 22 of the Book of Jeremiah and the book of 605 extends from chapter 1 to 25, but they must have been written later, since Jehoiachin (Coniah) did not reign until 598.

Jehoiachin Will Be Cast Out (22:24-27)

The first passage dates to just before the deportation of Jehoiachin. It uses the future tense: "I will cast thee out."

²²:²⁴As I live, saith the Lord, though Coniah the son of Jehoiakim king of Judah were the signet upon My right hand, yet would I pluck thee thence; ²⁵and I will give thee into the hand of them that seek thy life, and into the hand of them of whom thou art afraid, even into the hand of Nebuchadrezzar king of Babylon, and into the hand of the Chaldeans. ²⁶And I will cast thee out, and thy mother that bore thee, into another country, where ye were not born; and there shall ye die. ²⁷But to the land whereunto they long to return, thither shall they not return.

Jehoiachin Is Cast Out (22:28-30)

The second passage dates to just after the deportation of Jehoiachin. It uses the present tense: "... they ... are cast into the land which they know not."

²²:²⁸Is this man Coniah a despised, broken image? Is he a vessel wherein is no pleasure? Wherefore are they cast out, he and his seed, and are cast into the land which they know not?

²⁹O land, land, land, hear the word of the Lord. ³⁰Thus saith the Lord: Write ye this man childless, a man that shall not prosper in his days; for no man of his seed shall prosper, sitting upon the throne of David, and ruling any more in Judah.

Reign of Zedekiah: 597-586 BCE

In 597, Nebuchadnezzar's siege of Jerusalem succeeded. After deposing Jehoiachin, the son of Jehoiakim, he installed Zedekiah, the younger brother of Jehoiakim, as the new king, making Judah a vassal state of Babylon.

In 589, a new pharaoh began to reign in Egypt, Pharaoh Hophra. Zedekiah saw this as an opportunity to escape from Babylonian domination, and he approached the new pharaoh; as Ezekiel 17:15 says, "he [Zedekiah] rebelled against him [Nebuchadnezzar] in sending his ambassadors into Egypt, that they might give him horses and much people." The new Pharaoh agreed to support him, but Jeremiah remained convinced that Babylon would be the dominant power.

Nebuchadnezzar moved immediately to punish Judah's rebellion, and the punishment was much harsher than it had been for the earlier rebellion of Jehoiakim and Jehoiachin. This time, after taking Jerusalem, in 586 the Babylonians razed the city, destroyed its walls, burned the Temple, killed Zedekiah's sons while he watched, and then blinded Zedekiah and imprisoned him in Babylon. They sent most of Judah's people to exile in Babylon, allowing only the poor to remain. They appointed Gedaliah as governor, ruling the remnant on their behalf.

Jeremiah Wears a Yoke (27:1-28:17)

Early in the reign of Zedekiah, other prophets said that Judah should free itself from Babylon (27:9), and Jeremiah began to wear a yoke to emphasize that Judah should not try to break from the yoke of Babylonian domination. He prophesied that God had made Nebuchadnezzar ruler and that Judah would be destroyed completely if it tried to resist Babylon.

This passage begins with an error, saying it happened "[27:1]In the beginning of the reign of Jehoiakim," though it speaks two verses later of "[27:3]...Zedekiah king of Judah," and the rest of the story is also about the reign of Zedekiah. The mention of Jehoiakim is not in the Septuagint and is clearly a later addition that mistakenly said "Jehoiakim" instead of "Zedekiah."

We know that Jeremiah began wearing a yoke by the fourth year of Zedekiah's reign, because we learn later that "²⁸:¹ ... in the beginning of the reign of Zedekiah king of Judah, in the fourth year, in the fifth month," the prophet Hananiah broke the yoke that Jeremiah was wearing.

²⁷:¹In the beginning of the reign of Jehoiakim *[should be Zedekiah]* the son of Josiah, king of Judah, came this word unto Jeremiah from the Lord, saying: ²'Thus saith the Lord to me: Make thee bands and bars, and put them upon thy neck; ³and send them to the king of Edom, and to the king of Moab, and to the king of the children of Ammon, and to the king of Tyre, and to the king of Zidon, by the hand of the messengers that come to Jerusalem unto Zedekiah king of Judah; ⁴and give them a charge unto their masters, saying:

Thus saith the Lord of hosts, the God of Israel: Thus shall ye say unto your masters: ⁵I have made the earth, the man and the beast that are upon the face of the earth, by My great power and by My outstretched arm; and I give it unto whom it seemeth right unto Me. ⁶And now have I given all these lands into the hand of Nebuchadnezzar the king of Babylon, My servant; and the beasts of the field also have I given him to serve him. ⁷And all the nations shall serve him, and his son, and his son's son, until the time of his own land come; and then many nations and great kings shall make him their bondman. ⁸And it shall come to pass, that the nation and the kingdom which will not serve the same Nebuchadnezzar king of Babylon, and that will not put their neck under the yoke of the king of Babylon, that nation will I visit, saith the Lord, with the sword, and with the famine, and with the pestilence, until I have consumed them by his hand.

⁹But as for you, hearken ye not to your prophets, nor to your diviners, nor to your dreams, nor to your soothsayers, nor to your sorcerers, that speak unto you, saying: Ye shall not serve the king of Babylon; ¹⁰for they prophesy a lie unto you, to remove you far from

your land; and that I should drive you out and ye should perish. [11]But the nation that shall bring their neck under the yoke of the king of Babylon, and serve him, that nation will I let remain in their own land, saith the Lord; and they shall till it, and dwell therein.'

[12]And I spoke to Zedekiah king of Judah according to all these words, saying: 'Bring your necks under the yoke of the king of Babylon, and serve him and his people, and live. [13]Why will ye die, thou and thy people, by the sword, by the famine, and by the pestilence, as the Lord hath spoken concerning the nation that will not serve the king of Babylon? [14]And hearken not unto the words of the prophets that speak unto you, saying: Ye shall not serve the king of Babylon, for they prophesy a lie unto you. [15]For I have not sent them, saith the Lord, and they prophesy falsely in My name; that I might drive you out, and that ye might perish, ye, and the prophets that prophesy unto you.'

[16]Also I spoke to the priests and to all this people, saying: 'Thus saith the Lord: Hearken not to the words of your prophets that prophesy unto you, saying: Behold, the vessels of the Lord's house shall now shortly be brought back from Babylon; for they prophesy a lie unto you. [17]Hearken not unto them; serve the king of Babylon, and live; wherefore should this city become desolate? [18]But if they be prophets, and if the word of the Lord be with them, let them now make intercession to the Lord of hosts, that the vessels which are left in the house of the Lord, and in the house of the king of Judah, and at Jerusalem, go not to Babylon. [19]For thus saith the Lord of hosts concerning the pillars, and concerning the sea, and concerning the bases, and concerning the residue of the vessels that remain in this city, [20]which Nebuchadnezzar king of Babylon took not, when he carried away captive Jeconiah the son of Jehoiakim, king of Judah, from Jerusalem to Babylon, and all the nobles of Judah and Jerusalem; [21]yea, thus saith the Lord of hosts, the God of Israel, concerning the vessels that remain in the house of the Lord, and in the house of the king of Judah, and at Jerusalem: [22]They shall be carried to Babylon, and there shall they be, until the day that I remember them, saith the Lord, and bring them up, and restore them to this place.'

The controversy came to a head when Hananiah ben Azzur prophesied to a large crowd that Judah would break the yoke of Babylon, and after Jeremiah agreed with him, apparently intimidated by the crowd, Hananiah broke the yoke that Jeremiah was wearing. But Jeremiah soon changed his mind and denounced Hananiah, who died shortly afterwards.

28:1 And it came to pass the same year, in the beginning of the reign of Zedekiah king of Judah, in the fourth year, in the fifth month, that Hananiah the son of Azzur the prophet, who was of Gibeon, spoke unto me in the house of the Lord, in the presence of the priests and of all the people, saying: 2 'Thus speaketh the Lord of hosts, the God of Israel, saying: I have broken the yoke of the king of Babylon. 3 Within two full years will I bring back into this place all the vessels of the Lord's house, that Nebuchadnezzar king of Babylon took away from this place, and carried them to Babylon; 4 and I will bring back to this place Jeconiah the son of Jehoiakim, king of Judah, with all the captives of Judah, that went to Babylon, saith the Lord; for I will break the yoke of the king of Babylon.'

5 Then the prophet Jeremiah said unto the prophet Hananiah in the presence of the priests, and in the presence of all the people that stood in the house of the Lord, 6 even the prophet Jeremiah said: 'Amen! The Lord do so! The Lord perform thy words which thou hast prophesied, to bring back the vessels of the Lord's house, and all them that are carried away captive, from Babylon unto this place! 7 Nevertheless hear thou now this word that I speak in thine ears, and in the ears of all the people: 8 The prophets that have been before me and before thee of old prophesied against many countries, and against great kingdoms, of war, and of evil, and of pestilence. 9 The prophet that prophesieth of peace, when the word of the prophet shall come to pass, then shall the prophet be known, that the Lord hath truly sent him.'

10 Then Hananiah the prophet took the bar from off the prophet Jeremiah's neck, and broke it. 11 And Hananiah spoke in the presence of all the people, saying: 'Thus saith the Lord: Even so will I break the yoke of Nebuchadnezzar king of Babylon from off

the neck of all the nations within two full years.' And the prophet Jeremiah went his way.

¹²Then the word of the Lord came unto Jeremiah, after that Hananiah the prophet had broken the bar from off the neck of the prophet Jeremiah, saying: ¹³'Go, and tell Hananiah, saying: Thus saith the Lord: Thou hast broken the bars of wood; but thou shalt make in their stead bars of iron. ¹⁴For thus saith the Lord of hosts, the God of Israel: I have put a yoke of iron upon the neck of all these nations, that they may serve Nebuchadnezzar king of Babylon; and they shall serve him; and I have given him the beasts of the field also.' ¹⁵Then said the prophet Jeremiah unto Hananiah the prophet: 'Hear now, Hananiah; the Lord hath not sent thee; but thou makest this people to trust in a lie. ¹⁶'Therefore thus saith the Lord: Behold, I will send thee away from off the face of the earth; this year thou shalt die, because thou hast spoken perversion against the Lord.' ¹⁷So Hananiah the prophet died the same year in the seventh month.

The Good and Bad Figs (24:1-10)

Jeremiah prophesies that the first wave of exiles to Babylon will return to Judah but those who remain in Judah with Zedekiah will be destroyed. This passage was obviously written after Babylon exiled Jehoiachin and many prominent Judeans in 597, but it is hard to date it more precisely. Jeremiah had given up hope that those who remained in Judah would survive, but he now had hope that the future lay with the Judeans who were in exile.

"Chaldeans" is another name for Babylonians. Jeconiah was the original name of Jehoiachin. Though this passage is in the book of 605, it was clearly written later than that date, because it refers to the first Babylonian exile and to King Zedekiah.

²⁴:¹The Lord showed me, and behold two baskets of figs set before the temple of the Lord; after that Nebuchadrezzar king of Babylon had carried away captive Jeconiah the son of Jehoiakim, king of Judah, and the princes of Judah, with the craftsmen and smiths,

from Jerusalem, and had brought them to Babylon. ²One basket had very good figs, like the figs that are first-ripe; and the other basket had very bad figs, which could not be eaten, they were so bad. ³Then said the Lord unto me: 'What seest thou, Jeremiah?' And I said: 'Figs; the good figs, very good; and the bad, very bad, that cannot be eaten, they are so bad.'

⁴And the word of the Lord came unto me, saying: ⁵'Thus saith the Lord, the God of Israel: Like these good figs, so will I regard the captives of Judah, whom I have sent out of this place into the land of the Chaldeans, for good. ⁶And I will set Mine eyes upon them for good, and I will bring them back to this land; and I will build them, and not pull them down; and I will plant them, and not pluck them up. ⁷And I will give them a heart to know Me, that I am the Lord; and they shall be My people, and I will be their God; for they shall return unto Me with their whole heart.

⁸And as the bad figs, which cannot be eaten, they are so bad; surely thus saith the Lord: So will I make Zedekiah the king of Judah, and his princes, and the residue of Jerusalem, that remain in this land, and them that dwell in the land of Egypt; ⁹I will even make them a horror among all the kingdoms of the earth for evil; a reproach and a proverb, a taunt and a curse, in all places whither I shall drive them. ¹⁰And I will send the sword, the famine, and the pestilence, among them, till they be consumed from off the land that I gave unto them and to their fathers.'

Letter to the Exiles in Babylon (29:1-32)

After the first exile to Babylon, Jeremiah had no hope that the Judeans who remained would reform or even survive, but he did hope that the Judeans in exile would return.

The parable of the good and bad figs said that the Judeans who remain in Judah are like bad figs and would be destroyed, while those exiled to Babylon are like good figs and would be saved (24:1-10). This letter is connected with the parable of the figs and repeats its image, saying, "²⁹:¹⁷thus saith the Lord of hosts: Behold, I will ... make them like vile figs, that cannot be eaten, they are so bad."

Here Jeremiah advises the exiles about how to live in Babylon and tells them they will return after seventy years. In reality, Cyrus the Great of Persia conquered Babylon and gave the Jews permission to return fifty-nine years after this first exile, and Nehemiah led a massive return one hundred fifty-three years after the first exile. Seventy years is the typical human lifespan, and Jeremiah seems to be using this number to imply that exiles have no hope of returning in their own lifetimes, so they should try to build good lives in Babylon.

This letter was apparently preserved separately, as one of the documents that were collected to create the book of Jeremiah, but its place in the historical narrative is clear. Like the parable of the figs, it was obviously written after Babylon exiled Jehoiachin and many prominent Judeans, calling the exiled king Jeconiah rather than using the throne name Jehoiachin (29:1-2).

Ahab the son of Kolaiah, and Zedekiah the son of Maaseiah, mentioned in the final paragraph, apparently were prophets who supported Jehoiakim's resistance to Babylon, who Jeremiah says will be punished. This translation is a bit confusing because it uses the future tense ("²⁹:²¹ ... I will deliver them into the hand of Nebuchadrezzar...") though this letter was written after Jehoiakim and his supporters were taken to Babylon by Nebuchadnezzar. The translation is based on the Jewish text of the Bible, where this verse is traditionally read using the participle "noten" which means "giving," but when we look at only the consonants and ignore the vowels that were added later, we see that it was originally written as the past "natan," which means "He gave." It makes more sense to translate it based on the original meaning as, "²⁹:²¹Thus saith the Lord of hosts, the God of Israel, concerning Ahab the son of Kolaiah, and concerning Zedekiah the son of Maaseiah, who prophesy a lie unto you in My name: Behold, He delivered them into the hand of Nebuchadrezzar...."

²⁹:¹Now these are the words of the letter that Jeremiah the prophet sent from Jerusalem unto the residue of the elders of the captivity, and to the priests, and to the prophets, and to all the people, whom Nebuchadnezzar had carried away captive from Jerusalem

to Babylon, [2]after that Jeconiah the king, and the queen-mother, and the officers, and the princes of Judah and Jerusalem, and the craftsmen, and the smiths, were departed from Jerusalem; [3]by the hand of Elasah the son of Shaphan, and Gemariah the son of Hilkiah, whom Zedekiah king of Judah sent unto Babylon to Nebuchadnezzar king of Babylon, saying:

[4]Thus saith the Lord of hosts, the God of Israel, unto all the captivity, whom I have caused to be carried away captive from Jerusalem unto Babylon:

[5]Build ye houses, and dwell in them, and plant gardens, and eat the fruit of them; [6]take ye wives, and beget sons and daughters; and take wives for your sons, and give your daughters to husbands, that they may bear sons and daughters; and multiply ye there, and be not diminished. [7]And seek the peace of the city whither I have caused you to be carried away captive, and pray unto the Lord for it; for in the peace thereof shall ye have peace.

[8]For thus saith the Lord of hosts, the God of Israel: Let not your prophets that are in the midst of you, and your diviners, beguile you, neither hearken ye to your dreams which ye cause to be dreamed. [9]For they prophesy falsely unto you in My name; I have not sent them, saith the Lord. [10]For thus saith the Lord: After seventy years are accomplished for Babylon, I will remember you, and perform My good word toward you, in causing you to return to this place. [11]For I know the thoughts that I think toward you, saith the Lord, thoughts of peace, and not of evil, to give you a future and a hope. [12]And ye shall call upon Me, and go, and pray unto Me, and I will hearken unto you. [13]And ye shall seek Me, and find Me, when ye shall search for Me with all your heart. [14]And I will be found of you, saith the Lord, and I will turn your captivity, and gather you from all the nations, and from all the places whither I have driven you, saith the Lord; and I will bring you back unto the place whence I caused you to be carried away captive. [15]For ye have said: 'The Lord hath raised us up prophets in Babylon.'

[16]For thus saith the Lord concerning the king that sitteth upon the throne of David, and concerning all the people that dwell in this city, your brethren that are not gone forth with you into captivity; [17]thus saith the Lord of hosts: Behold, I will send upon them the

sword, the famine, and the pestilence, and will make them like vile figs, that cannot be eaten, they are so bad. [18]And I will pursue after them with the sword, with the famine, and with the pestilence, and will make them a horror unto all the kingdoms of the earth, a curse, and an astonishment, and a hissing, and a reproach, among all the nations whither I have driven them; [19]because they have not hearkened to My words, saith the Lord, wherewith I sent unto them My servants the prophets, sending them betimes and often; but ye would not hear, saith the Lord. [20]Hear ye therefore the word of the Lord, all ye of the captivity, whom I have sent away from Jerusalem to Babylon:

[21]Thus saith the Lord of hosts, the God of Israel, concerning Ahab the son of Kolaiah, and concerning Zedekiah the son of Maaseiah, who prophesy a lie unto you in My name: Behold, I will deliver [delivered] them into the hand of Nebuchadrezzar king of Babylon; and he shall slay them before your eyes; [22]and of them shall be taken up a curse by all the captivity of Judah that are in Babylon, saying: 'The Lord make thee like Zedekiah and like Ahab, whom the king of Babylon roasted in the fire'; [23]because they have wrought vile deeds in Israel, and have committed adultery with their neighbours' wives, and have spoken words in My name falsely, which I commanded them not; but I am He that knoweth, and am witness, saith the Lord.

The balance of the passage describes something that happened after the exiles received the letter. The people asked Shemaiah the Nehelamite why he had not criticized Jeremiah, and Jeremiah declared that Shemaiah the Nehelamite was a false prophet who would be punished. Judging from the passage, Shemaiah the Nehelamite had written letters to Jerusalem claiming that God made him the new priest instead of Jehoiada, and he predicted that the exile would be short, so the people thought he should have criticized Jeremiah's letter for saying that there would be a long exile of seventy years.

[29:24]And concerning Shemaiah the Nehelamite thou shalt speak, saying: [25]Thus speaketh the Lord of hosts, the God of Israel, saying: Because thou hast sent letters in thine own name unto all the people that are at Jerusalem, and to Zephaniah the son of Maaseiah the priest, and to all the priests, saying: [26]'The Lord hath made thee priest in the stead of Jehoiada the priest, that there should be officers in the house of the Lord for every man that is mad, and maketh himself a prophet, that thou shouldest put him in the stocks and in the collar. [27]Now therefore, why hast thou not rebuked Jeremiah of Anathoth, who maketh himself a prophet to you, [28]forasmuch as he hath sent unto us in Babylon, saying: The captivity is long; build ye houses, and dwell in them; and plant gardens, and eat the fruit of them?'

[29]And Zephaniah the priest read this letter in the ears of Jeremiah the prophet. [30]Then came the word of the Lord unto Jeremiah, saying: [31]Send to all them of the captivity, saying: Thus saith the Lord concerning Shemaiah the Nehelamite: Because that Shemaiah hath prophesied unto you, and I sent him not, and he hath caused you to trust in a lie; [32]therefore thus saith the Lord: Behold, I will punish Shemaiah the Nehelamite, and his seed; he shall not have a man to dwell among this people, neither shall he behold the good that I will do unto My people, saith the Lord; because he hath spoken perversion against the Lord.

Prophecy During the Siege—1 (21:1-10)

In 589, when Pharaoh Hophra began to reign in Egypt, Zedekiah decided to rebel against Babylon with the new pharaoh's help. Nebuchadnezzar responded by devastating Judah and besieging Jerusalem. Early in the Babylonian siege, according to this story, Zedekiah sent two representatives to Jeremiah to ask for his advice. Jeremiah replied that Zedekiah would be destroyed and that the Judeans should abandon him and surrender to the Babylonians (also called the Chaldeans).

This passage is in the Book of 605, as it is preserved in chapters 1-25 of the Book of Jeremiah, but it is clearly about an event that occurred after 605. Verse 21:1 dates it to the reign of

Zedekiah, and verse 21:4 dates it to a time when Jerusalem was being besieged.

There are three stories of Jeremiah prophesying destruction to Zedekiah during the siege: this passage (21:1-10) and the two passages that follow in this edition (34:1-6 and 37:1-10). It seems most likely that these are three accounts of one event, with different details. It does not seem plausible that they are separate events, that after Zedekiah asked Jeremiah for advice and received a prophecy of destruction (21:1-10), and after Jeremiah went to Zedekiah to deliver another prophecy of destruction (34:1-6), Zedekiah sent again to ask Jeremiah to pray for him, only to receive the yet another prophecy of destruction (37:1-10).

21:1The word which came unto Jeremiah from the Lord, when king Zedekiah sent unto him Pashhur the son of Malchiah, and Zephaniah the son of Maaseiah the priest, saying: 2'Inquire, I pray thee, of the Lord for us; for Nebuchadrezzar king of Babylon maketh war against us; peradventure the Lord will deal with us according to all His wondrous works, that he may go up from us.'

3Then said Jeremiah unto them: Thus shall ye say to Zedekiah: 4Thus saith the Lord, the God of Israel:

Behold, I will turn back the weapons of war that are in your hands, wherewith ye fight against the king of Babylon, and against the Chaldeans, that besiege you without the walls, and I will gather them into the midst of this city. 5And I myself will fight against you with an outstretched hand and with a strong arm, even in anger, and in fury, and in great wrath. 6And I will smite the inhabitants of this city, both man and beast; they shall die of a great pestilence. 7And afterward, saith the Lord, I will deliver Zedekiah king of Judah, and his servants, and the people, and such as are left in this city from the pestilence, from the sword, and from the famine, into the hand of Nebuchadrezzar king of Babylon, and into the hand of their enemies, and into the hand of those that seek their life; and he shall smite them with the edge of the sword; he shall not spare them, neither have pity, nor have compassion.

8And unto this people thou shalt say: Thus saith the Lord: Behold, I set before you the way of life and the way of death. 9He that abideth in this city shall die by the sword, and by the famine, and by the pestilence; but he that goeth out, and falleth away to the Chaldeans that besiege you, he shall live, and his life shall be unto him for a prey. [10]For I have set My face against this city for evil, and not for good, saith the Lord; it shall be given into the hand of the king of Babylon, and he shall burn it with fire.

Prophecy During the Siege—2 (34:1-6)

In this passage, from one of the books of incidents of Jeremiah's life, Jeremiah prophesies during the siege that Jerusalem will be destroyed and Zedekiah will be taken captive. In this, the second of the three accounts of prophecies to Zedekiah during the siege, Jeremiah goes to Zedekiah unbidden to deliver the prophecy, while in the other two, Zedekiah sends for Jeremiah. Verse 34:7 dates this passage to a time when Jerusalem and two other fortified cities had not been captured and were being besieged.

[34:1]The word which came unto Jeremiah from the Lord, when Nebuchadrezzar king of Babylon, and all his army, and all the kingdoms of the land of his dominion, and all the peoples, fought against Jerusalem, and against all the cities thereof, saying:

[2]Thus saith the Lord, the God of Israel: Go, and speak to Zedekiah king of Judah, and tell him: Thus saith the Lord: Behold, I will give this city into the hand of the king of Babylon, and he shall burn it with fire; [3]and thou shalt not escape out of his hand, but shalt surely be taken, and delivered into his hand; and thine eyes shall behold the eyes of the king of Babylon, and he shall speak with thee mouth to mouth, and thou shalt go to Babylon. [4]Yet hear the word of the Lord, O Zedekiah king of Judah: Thus saith the Lord concerning thee: Thou shalt not die by the sword; [5]thou shalt die in peace; and with the burnings of thy fathers, the former kings that were before thee, so shall they make a burning for thee; and they shall lament thee: 'Ah lord!' For I have spoken the word, saith the Lord.

[6]Then Jeremiah the prophet spoke all these words unto

Zedekiah king of Judah in Jerusalem, [7]when the king of Babylon's army fought against Jerusalem, and against all the cities of Judah that were left, against Lachish and against Azekah; for these alone remained of the cities of Judah as fortified cities.

Prophecy During the Siege—3 (37:1-10)

When the Egyptian army came to help Judah in 588, Nebuchadnezzar lifted the siege of Jerusalem temporarily and led his army to meet the Egyptians, and the Egyptians retreated without ever fighting the Babylonians. Verse 37:5 dates this passage to this time.

This passage is from one of the collections of incidents of Jeremiah's life, but it clearly was originally written as a separate text, since it begins by briefly recapping the beginning of Zedekiah's reign before talking about the Egyptian army coming and temporarily breaking the siege. Then it says that, while the siege was lifted, Zedekiah asked Jeremiah to pray for Judah, and Jeremiah responded by prophesying the destruction of Judah.

This is the third of the Jeremiah's three prophecies to Zedekiah during the siege, and it differs from the other two because it happened during the temporary lifting of the siege. Notice that, in the first, Zedekiah sends Pashhur the son of Malchiah, and Zephaniah the son of Maaseiah the priest to Jeremiah (21:1), and in this version, Zedekiah sends Jehucal the son of Shelemiah, and Zephaniah the son of Maaseiah the priest (37:3). These seem to be two versions of the same tradition, with one name preserved and one changed during transmission.

The name Coniah refers to Jehoiachin in this passage, as in chapter 23. Before the king adopted the throne name Jehoiachin, his name was Jeconiah, which is sometimes shortened to Coniah.

[37:1]And Zedekiah the son of Josiah reigned as king, instead of Coniah the son of Jehoiakim, whom Nebuchadnezzar king of Babylon made king in the land of Judah. [2]But neither he, nor his servants, nor the people of the land, did hearken unto the words of the Lord, which He spoke by the prophet Jeremiah.

³And Zedekiah the king sent Jehucal the son of Shelemiah, and Zephaniah the son of Maaseiah the priest, to the prophet Jeremiah, saying: 'Pray now unto the Lord our God for us.' ⁴Now Jeremiah came in and went out among the people; for they had not put him into prison. ⁵And Pharaoh's army was come forth out of Egypt; and when the Chaldeans that besieged Jerusalem heard tidings of them, they broke up from Jerusalem.

⁶Then came the word of the Lord unto the prophet Jeremiah, saying: ⁷'Thus saith the Lord, the God of Israel: Thus shall ye say to the king of Judah, that sent you unto Me to inquire of Me: Behold, Pharaoh's army, which is come forth to help you, shall return to Egypt into their own land. ⁸And the Chaldeans shall return, and fight against this city; and they shall take it, and burn it with fire. ⁹Thus saith the Lord: Deceive not yourselves, saying: The Chaldeans shall surely depart from us; for they shall not depart. ¹⁰For though ye had smitten the whole army of the Chaldeans that fight against you, and there remained but wounded men among them, yet would they rise up every man in his tent, and burn this city with fire.'

Freeing the Slaves (34:8-22)

During the time when the siege was temporarily lifted, Zedekiah proclaimed that all Judeans who were slaves should be freed, but after freeing them, their masters made them slaves again. In this passage from one of the books of incidents from Jeremiah's life, the prophet condemned them for violating the commandment that all Israelite slaves should be freed permanently every seventh year and prophesied that Babylon would punish them by destroying Judah.

Oddly, the commandment that has come down to us in Leviticus says that slaves should be freed every forty-nine years: every seventh year should be a sabbatical year when the fields are left fallow, and every seventh sabbatical year should be a jubilee year when slaves are freed (Lev 25:2-10). By contrast, an earlier law code that is preserved in Exodus says that male slaves should be freed every seventh year (Ex 21:2-5). Jeremiah seems to be mixing the texts by quoting the phrase "proclaim liberty" (Lev 25:10) from Leviticus several times to support freeing slaves every seven years, as commanded in Exodus.

We can date this passage to the time of the lifting of the siege, because it concludes by saying, "[22]Behold, I will command, saith the Lord, and cause them to return to this city; and they shall fight against it, and take it, and burn it with fire." Since he predicts that the opposing army will return, they must have left.

[34:8]The word that came unto Jeremiah from the Lord, after that the king Zedekiah had made a covenant with all the people that were at Jerusalem, to proclaim liberty unto them; [9]that every man should let his man-servant, and every man his maid-servant, being a Hebrew man or a Hebrew woman, go free; that none should make bondmen of them, even of a Jew his brother; [10]and all the princes and all the people hearkened, that had entered into the covenant to let every one his man-servant, and every one his maid-servant, go free, and not to make bondmen of them any more; they hearkened, and let them go; [11]but afterwards they turned, and caused the servants and the handmaids, whom they had let go free, to return, and brought them into subjection for servants and for handmaids; [12]therefore the word of the Lord came to Jeremiah from the Lord, saying:

[13]Thus saith the Lord, the God of Israel: I made a covenant with your fathers in the day that I brought them forth out of the land of Egypt, out of the house of bondage, saying: [14]'At the end of seven years ye shall let go every man his brother that is a Hebrew, that hath been sold unto thee, and hath served thee six years, thou shalt let him go free from thee'; but your fathers hearkened not unto Me, neither inclined their ear. [15]And ye were now turned, and had done that which is right in Mine eyes, in proclaiming liberty every man to his neighbour; and ye had made a covenant before Me in the house whereon My name is called; [16]but ye turned and profaned My name, and caused every man his servant, and every

man his handmaid, whom ye had let go free at their pleasure, to return; and ye brought them into subjection, to be unto you for servants and for handmaids.

[17]Therefore thus saith the Lord: Ye have not hearkened unto Me, to proclaim liberty, every man to his brother, and every man to his neighbour; behold, I proclaim for you a liberty, saith the Lord, unto the sword, unto the pestilence, and unto the famine; and I will make you a horror unto all the kingdoms of the earth.

[18]And I will give the men that have transgressed My covenant, that have not performed the words of the covenant which they made before Me, when they cut the calf in twain and passed between the parts thereof; [19]the princes of Judah, and the princes of Jerusalem, the officers, and the priests, and all the people of the land, that passed between the parts of the calf; [20]I will even give them into the hand of their enemies, and into the hand of them that seek their life; and their dead bodies shall be for food unto the fowls of the heaven, and to the beasts of the earth. [21]And Zedekiah king of Judah and his princes will I give into the hand of their enemies, and into the hand of them that seek their life, and into the hand of the king of Babylon's army, that are gone up from you.

[22]Behold, I will command, saith the Lord, and cause them to return to this city; and they shall fight against it, and take it, and burn it with fire; and I will make the cities of Judah a desolation, without inhabitant.

Jeremiah Imprisoned—1 (37:11-21, 38:14-28)

While the Babylonians suspended the siege to attack the Egyptians, Jeremiah was arrested and imprisoned. There are two accounts of his arrest and imprisonment with different details, which are intertwined in the text. Both accounts end with his being imprisoned in the court of the guard. These intertwined accounts begin at 37:11 and continue to the end of chapter 38. Then they are interrupted by the account of Jeremiah being freed from imprisonment by the Babylonian conquerors in 39:1-14. Then in 39:15-18, the narrative returns to the time when Jeremiah was still in prison.

The first version of his imprisonment says that Jeremiah left the city and was accused of defecting to the Babylonians. He was put in a dungeon in the house of Jonathan the scribe, but when he told King Zedekiah that he might die in the dungeon, the king moved him to the court of the guard to save his life, despite Jeremiah's hostile responses to the king. We know that 38:14-28 is a continuation of this version of the story, because it mentions Jeremiah's imprisonment in Jonathan's house (38:26).

This version includes yet another account of Zedekiah asking Jeremiah for advice (38:14-24).

37:11And it came to pass, that when the army of the Chaldeans was broken up from Jerusalem for fear of Pharaoh's army, 12then Jeremiah went forth out of Jerusalem to go into the land of Benjamin, to receive his portion there, in the midst of the people. 13And when he was in the gate of Benjamin, a captain of the ward was there, whose name was Irijah, the son of Shelemiah, the son of Hananiah; and he laid hold on Jeremiah the prophet, saying: 'Thou fallest away to the Chaldeans.' 14Then said Jeremiah: 'It is false; I fall not away to the Chaldeans'; but he hearkened not to him; so Irijah laid hold on Jeremiah, and brought him to the princes. 15And the princes were wroth with Jeremiah, and smote him, and put him in prison in the house of Jonathan the scribe; for they had made that the prison.

16When Jeremiah was come into the dungeon-house, and into the cells, and Jeremiah had remained there many days; 17then Zedekiah the king sent, and fetched him; and the king asked him secretly in his house, and said: 'Is there any word from the Lord?' And Jeremiah said: 'There is.' He said also: 'Thou shalt be delivered into the hand of the king of Babylon.' 18Moreover Jeremiah said unto king Zedekiah: 'Wherein have I sinned against thee, or against thy servants, or against this people, that ye have put me in prison? 19Where now are your prophets that prophesied unto you, saying: The king of Babylon shall not come against you, nor against this land? 20And now hear, I pray thee, O my lord the king: let my supplication, I pray thee, be presented before thee; that thou cause me not to return to the house of Jonathan the scribe, lest I die there.'

²¹Then Zedekiah the king commanded, and they committed Jeremiah into the court of the guard, and they gave him daily a loaf of bread out of the bakers' street, until all the bread in the city was spent. Thus Jeremiah remained in the court of the guard.

³⁸:¹⁴Then Zedekiah the king sent, and took Jeremiah the prophet unto him into the third entry that was in the house of the Lord; and the king said unto Jeremiah: 'I will ask thee a thing; hide nothing from me.' ¹⁵Then Jeremiah said unto Zedekiah: 'If I declare it unto thee, wilt thou not surely put me to death? And if I give thee counsel, thou wilt not hearken unto me.' ¹⁶So Zedekiah the king swore secretly unto Jeremiah, saying: 'As the Lord liveth, that made us this soul, I will not put thee to death, neither will I give thee into the hand of these men that seek thy life.'

¹⁷Then said Jeremiah unto Zedekiah: 'Thus saith the Lord, the God of hosts, the God of Israel: If thou wilt go forth unto the king of Babylon's princes, then thy soul shall live, and this city shall not be burned with fire; and thou shalt live, thou, and thy house; ¹⁸but if thou wilt not go forth to the king of Babylon's princes, then shall this city be given into the hand of the Chaldeans, and they shall burn it with fire, and thou shalt not escape out of their hand.'

¹⁹And Zedekiah the king said unto Jeremiah: 'I am afraid of the Jews that are fallen away to the Chaldeans, lest they deliver me into their hand, and they mock me.'

²⁰But Jeremiah said: 'They shall not deliver thee. Hearken, I beseech thee, to the voice of the Lord, in that which I speak unto thee; so it shall be well with thee, and thy soul shall live.

²¹But if thou refuse to go forth, this is the word that the Lord hath shown me: ²²Behold, all the women that are left in the king of Judah's house shall be brought forth to the king of Babylon's princes, and those women shall say: 'Thy familiar friends have set thee on, And have prevailed over thee; Thy feet are sunk in the mire, And they are turned away back.' ²³And they shall bring out all thy wives and thy children to the Chaldeans; and thou shalt not escape out of their hand, but shalt be taken by the hand of the king of Babylon; and thou shalt cause this city to be burned with fire.'

²⁴Then said Zedekiah unto Jeremiah: 'Let no man know of

these words, and thou shalt not die. [25]But if the princes hear that I have talked with thee, and they come unto thee, and say unto thee: Declare unto us now what thou hast said unto the king; hide it not from us, and we will not put thee to death; also what the king said unto thee; [26]then thou shalt say unto them: I presented my supplication before the king, that he would not cause me to return to Jonathan's house, to die there.'

[27]Then came all the princes unto Jeremiah, and asked him; and he told them according to all these words that the king had commanded. So they left off speaking with him; for the matter was not reported. [28]So Jeremiah abode in the court of the guard until the day that Jerusalem was taken.

Jeremiah Imprisoned—2 (38:1-13, 39:15-18)

The second version of this story says that Jeremiah was imprisoned because his prophecies that Judah would be destroyed were hurting the morale of Judah's soldiers and people. He was imprisoned in a dungeon that was a pit under the court of the guard, but he was taken out of the pit when Ebed-melech the Ethiopian told the king he would die there. We know that 39:15-18 is a continuation of this account, because it says Ebed-melech will be spared when Jerusalem is destroyed.

This passage follows from the following statement in the first version of Jeremiah's prophecy to Zedekiah during the siege: "[21:8]And unto this people thou shalt say: Thus saith the Lord: Behold, I set before you the way of life and the way of death. [9]He that abideth in this city shall die by the sword, and by the famine, and by the pestilence; but he that goeth out, and falleth away to the Chaldeans that besiege you, he shall live...." Now, Jeremiah is following this commandment and actively telling the people to defect to the Babylonians.

[38:1]And Shephatiah the son of Mattan, and Gedaliah the son of Pashhur, and Jucal the son of Shelemiah, and Pashhur the son of

Malchiah, heard the words that Jeremiah spoke unto all the people, saying: [2]'Thus saith the Lord: He that remaineth in this city shall die by the sword, by the famine, and by the pestilence; but he that goeth forth to the Chaldeans shall live, and his life shall be unto him for a prey, and he shall live. [3]Thus saith the Lord: This city shall surely be given into the hand of the army of the king of Babylon, and he shall take it.'

[4]Then the princes said unto the king: 'Let this man, we pray thee, be put to death; forasmuch as he weakeneth the hands of the men of war that remain in this city, and the hands of all the people, in speaking such words unto them; for this man seeketh not the welfare of this people, but the hurt.' [5]Then Zedekiah the king said: 'Behold, he is in your hand; for the king is not he that can do any thing against you.' [6]Then took they Jeremiah, and cast him into the pit of Malchiah the king's son, that was in the court of the guard; and they let down Jeremiah with cords. And in the pit there was no water, but mire; and Jeremiah sank in the mire.

[7]Now when Ebed-melech the Ethiopian, an officer, who was in the king's house, heard that they had put Jeremiah in the pit; the king then sitting in the gate of Benjamin; [8]Ebed-melech went forth out of the king's house, and spoke to the king, saying: [9]'My lord the king, these men have done evil in all that they have done to Jeremiah the prophet, whom they have cast into the pit; and he is like to die in the place where he is because of the famine; for there is no more bread in the city.' [10]Then the king commanded Ebed-melech the Ethiopian, saying: 'Take from hence thirty men with thee, and take up Jeremiah the prophet out of the pit, before he die.' [11]So Ebed-melech took the men with him, and went into the house of the king under the treasury, and took thence worn clouts and worn rags, and let them down by cords into the pit to Jeremiah. [12]And Ebed-melech the Ethiopian said unto Jeremiah: 'Put now these worn clouts and rags under thine armholes under the cords.' And Jeremiah did so. [13]So they drew up Jeremiah with the cords, and took him up out of the pit; and Jeremiah remained in the court of the guard.

39:15Now the word of the Lord came unto Jeremiah, while he was shut up in the court of the guard, saying: 16'Go, and speak to Ebed-melech the Ethiopian, saying: Thus saith the Lord of hosts, the God of Israel: Behold, I will bring My words upon this city for evil, and not for good; and they shall be accomplished before thee in that day. 17But I will deliver thee in that day, saith the Lord; and thou shalt not be given into the hand of the men of whom thou art afraid. 18For I will surely deliver thee, and thou shalt not fall by the sword, but thy life shall be for a prey unto thee; because thou hast put thy trust in Me, saith the Lord.'

After the Fall of Jerusalem

When Nebuchadnezzar's second siege of Jerusalem succeeded, the Babylonian army razed the city, destroyed its walls, and exiled Judah to Babylon, leaving only the "39:10 ... the poor of the people, that had nothing, in the land of Judah," giving farms to these poor people, and appointing Gedaliah as their governor. Nebuchadnezzar let Jeremiah stay in Judah under the protection of Gedaliah, perhaps as a reward for his support of Babylon. Soon afterwards, the king of Ammon sent a member of his family to assassinate Gedaliah. The remaining Judean farmers fled to Egypt to escape the Ammonites, taking Jeremiah and Baruch with them, and leading Jeremiah to prophesy that Babylon would invade and destroy the Judeans in Egypt.

All Judah Is Carried Away (13:18-27)

This passage refers to the destruction and exile at the end of Zedekiah's reign, since it says "13:19... Judah is carried away captive all of it; it is wholly carried away captive." Though it is from the book of 605, it is clearly about an event that happened after that date.

13:18Say thou unto the king and to the queen-mother: 'Sit ye down low; for your headtires are come down, even your beautiful crown.' 19The cities of the South are shut up, and there is none to open them; Judah is carried away captive all of it; it is wholly carried away captive.

20Lift up your eyes, and behold them that come from the north; where is the flock that was given thee, thy beautiful flock? 21What wilt thou say, when He shall set the friends over thee as head, whom thou thyself hast trained against thee? Shall not pangs take hold of thee, As of a woman in travail? 22And if thou say in thy heart: 'Wherefore are these things befallen me?'—For the greatness of thine iniquity are thy skirts uncovered, and thy heels suffer violence.

23Can the Ethiopian change his skin, or the leopard his spots? Then may ye also do good, that are accustomed to do evil.

24Therefore will I scatter them, as the stubble that passeth away by the wind of the wilderness.

25This is thy lot, the portion measured unto thee from Me, saith the Lord; because thou hast forgotten Me, and trusted in falsehood. 26Therefore will I also uncover thy skirts upon thy face, and thy shame shall appear. 27Thine adulteries, and thy neighings, the lewdness of thy harlotry, on the hills in the field have I seen thy detestable acts. Woe unto thee, O Jerusalem! Thou wilt not be made clean! When shall it ever be?

Jeremiah is Spared (38:28b-39:11)

This passage, from the second collection of incidents in Jeremiah's life, begins by describing the fall of Jerusalem after a siege that lasted over a year and then describes Nebuchadnezzar's merciful treatment of Jeremiah.

38:28bAnd it came to pass, when Jerusalem was taken—39:1in the ninth year of Zedekiah king of Judah, in the tenth month, came Nebuchadrezzar king of Babylon and all his army against Jerusalem, and besieged it; 2in the eleventh year of Zedekiah, in the fourth month, the ninth day of the month, a breach was made in the city—³that all the princes of the king of Babylon came in, and sat in the middle gate, even Nergal-sarezer, Samgar-nebo, Sarsechim Rab-saris, Nergal-sarezer Rab-mag, with all the residue of the princes of the king of Babylon.

⁴And it came to pass, that when Zedekiah the king of Judah and all the men of war saw them, then they fled, and went forth out of the city by night, by the way of the king's garden, by the gate betwixt the two walls; and he went out the way of the Arabah. ⁵But the army of the Chaldeans pursued after them, and overtook Zedekiah in the plains of Jericho; and when they had taken him, they brought him up to Nebuchadrezzar king of Babylon to Riblah in the land of Hamath, and he gave judgment upon him. ⁶Then the king of Babylon slew the sons of Zedekiah in Riblah before his eyes; also the king of Babylon slew all the nobles of Judah. ⁷Moreover he put out Zedekiah's eyes, and bound him in fetters, to carry him to Babylon. ⁸And the Chaldeans burned the king's house, and the house of the people, with fire, and broke down the walls of Jerusalem.

⁹Then Nebuzaradan the captain of the guard carried away captive into Babylon the remnant of the people that remained in the city, the deserters also, that fell away to him, with the rest of the people that remained. ¹⁰But Nebuzaradan the captain of the guard left of the poor of the people, that had nothing, in the land of Judah, and gave them vineyards and fields in that day.

¹¹Now Nebuchadrezzar king of Babylon gave charge concerning Jeremiah to Nebuzaradan the captain of the guard, saying: ¹²'Take him, and look well to him, and do him no harm; but do unto him even as he shall say unto thee.' ¹³So Nebuzaradan the captain of the guard sent, and Nebushazban Rab-saris, and Nergal-sarezer Rab-mag, and all the chief officers of the king of Babylon; ¹⁴they sent, and took Jeremiah out of the court of the guard, and committed him unto Gedaliah the son of Ahikam, the son of Shaphan, that he should carry him home; so he dwelt among the people.

Judeans Flee to Egypt (40:1-43:7)

This passage gives more details about how Jeremiah was spared from exile. Needless to say, the captain's explanation of why Judah was defeated (40:2-3) is the writer's editorializing rather than what the captain actually might have said.

The passage goes on to say that, when the Jews who had fled to Moab and Ammon, east of the Jordan River, heard about Gedaliah, they returned to Judah. But the Ammonite Ishmael ben Nethaniah treacherously killed Gedaliah and other Judeans. The Judean remnant asked Jeremiah for advice, he told them to stay in Judah rather than fleeing to Egypt, but the Judeans did not believe him and fled to Egypt, taking Jeremiah and Baruch with them.

40:1The word which came to Jeremiah from the Lord, after that Nebuzaradan the captain of the guard had let him go from Ramah, when he had taken him being bound in chains among all the captives of Jerusalem and Judah, that were carried away captive unto Babylon.

2And the captain of the guard took Jeremiah, and said unto him: 'The Lord thy God pronounced this evil upon this place; 3and the Lord hath brought it, and done according as He spoke; because ye have sinned against the Lord, and have not hearkened to His voice, therefore this thing is come upon you. 4And now, behold, I loose thee this day from the chains which are upon thy hand. If it seem good unto thee to come with me into Babylon, come, and I will look well unto thee; but if it seem ill unto thee to come with me into Babylon, forbear; behold, all the land is before thee; whither it seemeth good and right unto thee to go, thither go.—5Yet he would not go back.—Go back then to Gedaliah the son of Ahikam, the son of Shaphan, whom the king of Babylon hath made governor over the cities of Judah, and dwell with him among the people; or go wheresoever it seemeth right unto thee to go.' So the captain of the guard gave him an allowance and a present, and let him go.

6Then went Jeremiah unto Gedaliah the son of Ahikam to Mizpah, and dwelt with him among the people that were left in the land.

[7]Now when all the captains of the forces that were in the fields, even they and their men, heard that the king of Babylon had made Gedaliah the son of Ahikam governor in the land, and had committed unto him men, and women, and children, and of the poorest of the land, of them that were not carried away captive to Babylon; [8]then they came to Gedaliah to Mizpah, even Ishmael the son of Nethaniah, and Johanan and Jonathan the sons of Kareah, and Seraiah the son of Tanhumeth, and the sons of Ephai the Netophathite, and Jezaniah the son of the Maacathite, they and their men. [9]And Gedaliah the son of Ahikam the son of Shaphan swore unto them and to their men, saying: 'Fear not to serve the Chaldeans; dwell in the land, and serve the king of Babylon, and it shall be well with you. [10]As for me, behold, I will dwell at Mizpah, to stand before the Chaldeans that may come unto us; but ye, gather ye wine and summer fruits and oil, and put them in your vessels, and dwell in your cities that ye have taken.'

[11]Likewise when all the Jews that were in Moab, and among the children of Ammon, and in Edom, and that were in all the countries, heard that the king of Babylon had left a remnant of Judah, and that he had set over them Gedaliah the son of Ahikam, the son of Shaphan; [12]then all the Jews returned out of all places whither they were driven, and came to the land of Judah, to Gedaliah, unto Mizpah, and gathered wine and summer fruits in great abundance.

[13]Moreover Johanan the son of Kareah, and all the captains of the forces that were in the fields, came to Gedaliah to Mizpah, [14]and said unto him: 'Dost thou know that Baalis the king of the children of Ammon hath sent Ishmael the son of Nethaniah to take thy life?' But Gedaliah the son of Ahikam believed them not. [15]Then Johanan the son of Kareah spoke to Gedaliah in Mizpah secretly, saying: 'Let me go, I pray thee, and I will slay Ishmael the son of Nethaniah, and no man shall know it; wherefore should he take thy life, that all the Jews that are gathered unto thee should be scattered, and the remnant of Judah perish?' [16]But Gedaliah the son of Ahikam said unto Johanan the son of Kareah: 'Thou shalt not do this thing; for thou speakest falsely of Ishmael.'

[41:1]Now it came to pass in the seventh month, that Ishmael the son of Nethaniah, the son of Elishama, of the seed royal, and one of the chief officers of the king, and ten men with him, came unto Gedaliah the son of Ahikam to Mizpah; and there they did eat bread together in Mizpah. [2]Then arose Ishmael the son of Nethaniah, and the ten men that were with him, and smote Gedaliah the son of Ahikam the son of Shaphan with the sword, and slew him, whom the king of Babylon had made governor over the land. [3]Ishmael also slew all the Jews that were with him, even with Gedaliah, at Mizpah, and the Chaldeans that were found there, even the men of war.

[4]And it came to pass the second day after he had slain Gedaliah, and no man knew it, [5]that there came certain men from Shechem, from Shiloh, and from Samaria, even fourscore men, having their beards shaven and their clothes rent, and having cut themselves, with meal-offerings and frankincense in their hand to bring them to the house of the Lord. [6]And Ishmael the son of Nethaniah went forth from Mizpah to meet them, weeping all along as he went; and it came to pass, as he met them, he said unto them: 'Come to Gedaliah the son of Ahikam.' [7]And it was so, when they came into the midst of the city, that Ishmael the son of Nethaniah slew them, and cast them into the midst of the pit, he, and the men that were with him. [8]But ten men were found among them that said unto Ishmael: 'Slay us not; for we have stores hidden in the field, of wheat, and of barley, and of oil, and of honey.' So he forbore, and slew them not among their brethren.

[9]Now the pit wherein Ishmael cast all the dead bodies of the men whom he had slain by the side of Gedaliah was that which Asa the king had made for fear of Baasa king of Israel; the same Ishmael the son of Nethaniah filled with them that were slain. [10]Then Ishmael carried away captive all the residue of the people that were in Mizpah, even the king's daughters, and all the people that remained in Mizpah, whom Nebuzaradan the captain of the guard had committed to Gedaliah the son of Ahikam; Ishmael the son of Nethaniah carried them away captive, and departed to go over to the children of Ammon.

[11]But when Johanan the son of Kareah, and all the captains of the forces that were with him, heard of all the evil that Ishmael the son of Nethaniah had done, [12]then they took all the men, and went to fight with Ishmael the son of Nethaniah, and found him by the great waters that are in Gibeon. [13]Now it came to pass, that when all the people that were with Ishmael saw Johanan the son of Kareah, and all the captains of the forces that were with him, then they were glad. [14]So all the people that Ishmael had carried away captive from Mizpah cast about and returned, and went unto Johanan the son of Kareah. [15]But Ishmael the son of Nethaniah escaped from Johanan with eight men, and went to the children of Ammon. [16]Then took Johanan the son of Kareah, and all the captains of the forces that were with him, all the remnant of the people whom he had recovered from Ishmael the son of Nethaniah, from Mizpah, after that he had slain Gedaliah the son of Ahikam, the men, even the men of war, and the women, and the children, and the officers, whom he had brought back from Gibeon; [17]and they departed, and dwelt in Geruth Chimham, which is by Beth-lehem, to go to enter into Egypt, [18]because of the Chaldeans; for they were afraid of them, because Ishmael the son of Nethaniah had slain Gedaliah the son of Ahikam, whom the king of Babylon made governor over the land.

[42:1]Then all the captains of the forces, and Johanan the son of Kareah, and Jezaniah the son of Hoshaiah, and all the people from the least even unto the greatest, came near, [2]and said unto Jeremiah the prophet: 'Let, we pray thee, our supplication be accepted before thee, and pray for us unto the Lord thy God, even for all this remnant; for we are left but a few of many, as thine eyes do behold us; [3]that the Lord thy God may tell us the way wherein we should walk, and the thing that we should do.' [4]Then Jeremiah the prophet said unto them: 'I have heard you; behold, I will pray unto the Lord your God according to your words; and it shall come to pass, that whatsoever thing the Lord shall answer you, I will declare it unto you; I will keep nothing back from you.' [5]Then they said to Jeremiah: 'The Lord be a true and faithful witness against us, if we do not even according to all the word wherewith the Lord thy God shall send thee to us. [6]Whether it be good, or whether it be evil, we will hearken to the voice of the Lord our God, to whom we send thee; that it may be well with us, when we hearken to the voice of the Lord our God.'

[7]And it came to pass after ten days, that the word of the Lord came unto Jeremiah. [8]Then called he Johanan the son of Kareah, and all the captains of the forces that were with him, and all the people from the least even to the greatest, [9]and said unto them: 'Thus saith the Lord, the God of Israel, unto whom ye sent me to present your supplication before Him: [10]If ye will still abide in this land, then will I build you, and not pull you down, and I will plant you, and not pluck you up; for I repent Me of the evil that I have done unto you. [11]Be not afraid of the king of Babylon, of whom ye are afraid; be not afraid of him, saith the Lord; for I am with you to save you, and to deliver you from his hand. [12]And I will grant you compassion, that he may have compassion upon you, and cause you to return to your own land.

[13]But if ye say: We will not abide in this land; so that ye hearken not to the voice of the Lord your God; [14]saying: No; but we will go into the land of Egypt, where we shall see no war, nor hear the sound of the horn, nor have hunger of bread; and there will we abide; [15]now therefore hear ye the word of the Lord, O remnant of Judah: Thus saith the Lord of hosts, the God of Israel: If ye wholly set your faces to enter into Egypt, and go to sojourn there; [16]then it shall come to pass, that the sword, which ye fear, shall overtake you there in the land of Egypt, and the famine, whereof ye are afraid, shall follow hard after you there in Egypt; and there ye shall die. [17]So shall it be with all the men that set their faces to go into Egypt to sojourn there; they shall die by the sword, by the famine, and by the pestilence; and none of them shall remain or escape from the evil that I will bring upon them. [18]For thus saith the Lord of hosts, the God of Israel: As Mine anger and My fury hath been poured forth upon the inhabitants of Jerusalem, so shall My fury be poured forth upon you, when ye shall enter into Egypt; and ye shall be an execration, and an astonishment, and a curse, and a reproach; and ye shall see this place no more. [19]The Lord

hath spoken concerning you, O remnant of Judah: Go ye not into Egypt; know certainly that I have forewarned you this day. [20]For ye have dealt deceitfully against your own souls; for ye sent me unto the Lord your God, saying: Pray for us unto the Lord our God; and according unto all that the Lord our God shall say, so declare unto us, and we will do it; [21]and I have this day declared it to you; but ye have not hearkened to the voice of the Lord your God in any thing for which He hath sent me unto you. [22]Now therefore know certainly that ye shall die by the sword, by the famine, and by the pestilence, in the place whither ye desire to go to sojourn there.'

[43:1]And it came to pass, that when Jeremiah had made an end of speaking unto all the people all the words of the Lord their God, wherewith the Lord their God had sent him to them, even all these words, [2]then spoke Azariah the son of Hoshaiah, and Johanan the son of Kareah, and all the proud men, saying unto Jeremiah: 'Thou speakest falsely; the Lord our God hath not sent thee to say: Ye shall not go into Egypt to sojourn there; [3]but Baruch the son of Neriah setteth thee on against us, to deliver us into the hand of the Chaldeans, that they may put us to death, and carry us away captives to Babylon.' [4]So Johanan the son of Kareah, and all the captains of the forces, and all the people, hearkened not to the voice of the Lord, to dwell in the land of Judah. [5]But Johanan the son of Kareah, and all the captains of the forces, took all the remnant of Judah, that were returned from all the nations whither they had been driven to sojourn in the land of Judah: [6]the men, and the women, and the children, and the king's daughters, and every person that Nebuzaradan the captain of the guard had left with Gedaliah the son of Ahikam, the son of Shaphan, and Jeremiah the prophet, and Baruch the son of Neriah; [7]and they came into the land of Egypt; for they hearkened not to the voice of the Lord; and they came even to Tahpanhes.

Prophecy of Destruction of Egypt (43:8-44:30)

After the Judeans took Jeremiah with them to Tahpanhes in Egypt, Jeremiah prophesied that Babylon would destroy Egypt, still convinced that Babylon will be the dominant power, as he had been since the beginning of Jehoiakim's reign. In fact, Nebuchadnezzar invaded Egypt in 568, but little is known about this invasion.

Jeremiah also condemned the Judeans who fled to Egypt for worshiping other gods, and when they replied that they would continue to worship other gods, he prophesied that they would be destroyed.

This is the end of the historical narrative, and it is fitting that it ends with a prophecy of destruction of those who worship other gods.

⁴³:⁸Then came the word of the Lord unto Jeremiah in Tahpanhes, saying: ⁹'Take great stones in thy hand, and hide them in the mortar in the framework, which is at the entry of Pharaoh's house in Tahpanhes, in the sight of the men of Judah; ¹⁰and say unto them: Thus saith the Lord of hosts, the God of Israel: Behold, I will send and take Nebuchadrezzar the king of Babylon, My servant, and will set his throne upon these stones that I have hid; and he shall spread his royal pavilion over them. ¹¹And he shall come, and shall smite the land of Egypt; such as are for death to death, and such as are for captivity to captivity, and such as are for the sword to the sword. ¹²And I will kindle a fire in the houses of the gods of Egypt; and he shall burn them, and carry them away captives; and he shall fold up the land of Egypt, as a shepherd foldeth up his garment; and he shall go forth from thence in peace. ¹³He shall also break the pillars of Beth-shemesh, that is in the land of Egypt; and the houses of the gods of Egypt shall he burn with fire.'

⁴⁴:¹The word that came to Jeremiah concerning all the Jews that dwelt in the land of Egypt, that dwelt at Migdol, and at Tahpanhes, and at Noph, and in the country of Pathros, saying: ²'Thus saith the Lord of hosts, the God of Israel: Ye have seen all the evil that I have brought upon Jerusalem, and upon all the cities of Judah; and, behold, this day they are a desolation, and no man dwelleth therein; ³because of their wickedness which they have committed to provoke Me, in that they went to offer, and to serve other gods, whom they knew not, neither they, nor ye, nor your fathers. ⁴Howbeit I sent unto you all My servants the prophets, sending

them betimes and often, saying: Oh, do not this abominable thing that I hate. [5]But they hearkened not, nor inclined their ear to turn from their wickedness, to forbear offering unto other gods. [6]Wherefore My fury and Mine anger was poured forth, and was kindled in the cities of Judah and in the streets of Jerusalem; and they are wasted and desolate, as at this day.

[7]Therefore now thus saith the Lord, the God of hosts, the God of Israel: Wherefore commit ye this great evil against your own souls, to cut off from you man and woman, infant and suckling, out of the midst of Judah, to leave you none remaining; [8]in that ye provoke Me with the works of your hands, offering unto other gods in the land of Egypt, whither ye are gone to sojourn; that ye may be cut off, and that ye may be a curse and a reproach among all the nations of the earth? [9]Have ye forgotten the wicked deeds of your fathers, and the wicked deeds of the kings of Judah, and the wicked deeds of their wives, and your own wicked deeds, and the wicked deeds of your wives, which they committed in the land of Judah, and in the streets of Jerusalem? [10]They are not humbled even unto this day, neither have they feared, nor walked in My law, nor in My statutes, that I set before you and before your fathers.

[11]Therefore thus saith the Lord of hosts, the God of Israel: Behold, I will set My face against you for evil, even to cut off all Judah. [12]And I will take the remnant of Judah, that have set their faces to go into the land of Egypt to sojourn there, and they shall all be consumed; in the land of Egypt shall they fall; they shall be consumed by the sword and by the famine; they shall die, from the least even unto the greatest, by the sword and by the famine; and they shall be an execration, and an astonishment, and a curse, and a reproach. [13]For I will punish them that dwell in the land of Egypt, as I have punished Jerusalem, by the sword, by the famine, and by the pestilence; [14]so that none of the remnant of Judah, that are gone into the land of Egypt to sojourn there, shall escape or remain, that they should return into the land of Judah, to which they have a desire to return to dwell there; for none shall return save such as shall escape.'

[15]Then all the men who knew that their wives offered unto other

gods, and all the women that stood by, a great assembly, even all the people that dwelt in the land of Egypt, in Pathros, answered Jeremiah, saying: [16]'As for the word that thou hast spoken unto us in the name of the Lord, we will not hearken unto thee. [17]But we will certainly perform every word that is gone forth out of our mouth, to offer unto the queen of heaven, and to pour out drink-offerings unto her, as we have done, we and our fathers, our kings and our princes, in the cities of Judah, and in the streets of Jerusalem; for then had we plenty of food, and were well, and saw no evil. [18]But since we let off to offer to the queen of heaven, and to pour out drink-offerings unto her, we have wanted all things, and have been consumed by the sword and by the famine. [19]And is it we that offer to the queen of heaven, and pour out drink-offerings unto her? Did we make her cakes in her image, and pour out drink-offerings unto her, without our husbands?'

[20]Then Jeremiah said unto all the people, to the men, and to the women, even to all the people that had given him that answer, saying: [21]'The offering that ye offered in the cities of Judah, and in the streets of Jerusalem, ye and your fathers, your kings and your princes, and the people of the land, did not the Lord remember them, and came it not into His mind? [22]So that the Lord could no longer bear, because of the evil of your doings, and because of the abominations which ye have committed; therefore is your land become a desolation, and an astonishment, and a curse, without an inhabitant, as at this day. [23]Because ye have offered, and because ye have sinned against the Lord, and have not hearkened to the voice of the Lord, nor walked in His law, nor in His statutes, nor in His testimonies; therefore this evil is happened unto you, as at this day.'

[24]Moreover Jeremiah said unto all the people, and to all the women: 'Hear the word of the Lord, all Judah that are in the land of Egypt: [25]Thus saith the Lord of hosts, the God of Israel, saying: Ye and your wives have both spoken with your mouths, and with your hands have fulfilled it, saying: We will surely perform our vows that we have vowed, to offer to the queen of heaven, and to pour out drink-offerings unto her; ye shall surely establish your

vows, and surely perform your vows. [26]Therefore hear ye the word of the Lord, all Judah that dwell in the land of Egypt: Behold, I have sworn by My great name, saith the Lord, that My name shall no more be named in the mouth of any man of Judah in all the land of Egypt saying: As the Lord God liveth. [27]Behold, I watch over them for evil, and not for good; and all the men of Judah that are in the land of Egypt shall be consumed by the sword and by the famine, until there be an end of them. [28]And they that escape the sword shall return out of the land of Egypt into the land of Judah, few in number; and all the remnant of Judah, that are gone into the land of Egypt to sojourn there, shall know whose word shall stand, Mine, or theirs. [29]And this shall be the sign unto you, saith the Lord, that I will punish you in this place, that ye may know that My words shall surely stand against you for evil; [30]thus saith the Lord: Behold, I will give Pharaoh Hophra king of Egypt into the hand of his enemies, and into the hand of them that seek his life; as I gave Zedekiah king of Judah into the hand of Nebuchadrezzar king of Babylon, his enemy, and that sought his life.'

The Book of 605
(Chapters 1-25)

This section includes passages from the Book of 605 that are not included in the historical narrative, either because they cannot be dated or because they are not authentic. About one-third of the passages from the Book of 605 are included in the historical narrative, and about two-thirds are in this section, listed in the same order in which they appear in the Book of Jeremiah.

The passages that cannot be dated are often prophecies of destruction that could have come at many times in Jeremiah's career. Removing these from the historical narrative makes the narrative easier to follow, but it also means that the narrative does not present a complete picture of Jeremiah. If we want to understand what Jeremiah was like, we have to imagine inserting these prophecies of destruction throughout his career—in addition to the prophecies of destruction that are in the historical narrative.

Prophecy of Destruction (4:5-13, 4:15-6:7, 6:9-15)

Based on verse 4:5, this prophecy of destruction was written when Judah retreated to its fortified cities during one of the Babylonian attacks, but we cannot say whether it refers to the siege in Jehoiakim's time or in Zedekiah's time.

Verses 4:14 and 6:8 are omitted because these are the conclusion of a prophecy from early in the reign of Josiah where Jeremiah's calls on Judah and Israel to repent. This early passage was intertwined with the passage here, which comes from a later period after Jeremiah gave up hope of Judah repenting.

The verse, "⁴·¹⁵For hark! One declareth from Dan, and announceth calamity from the hills of Ephraim" uses the two tribes, Dan and Ephraim, to represent all of the northern kingdom of Israel, warning Judah that it will be destroyed as Israel was.

Notice that this passage includes moral sins as well as the religious sin of idol worship: "⁵·²⁸They plead not the cause, the cause of the fatherless, that they might make it to prosper; and the right of the needy do they not judge."

⁴·⁵Declare ye in Judah, and publish in Jerusalem, and say: 'Blow ye the horn in the land'; cry aloud and say: 'Assemble yourselves, and let us go into the fortified cities.' ⁶Set up a standard toward Zion; put yourselves under covert, stay not; for I will bring evil from the north, and a great destruction.

⁷A lion is gone up from his thicket, and a destroyer of nations Is set out, gone forth from his place; to make thy land desolate, that thy cities be laid waste, without inhabitant. ⁸For this gird you with sackcloth, lament and wail; for the fierce anger of the Lord is not turned back from us.

⁹And it shall come to pass at that day, saith the Lord, that the heart of the king shall fail, and the heart of the princes; and the priests shall be astonished, and the prophets shall wonder.

¹⁰Then said I: 'Ah, Lord God! Surely Thou hast greatly deceived this people and Jerusalem, saying: Ye shall have peace; whereas the sword reacheth unto the soul.'

¹¹At that time shall it be said of this people and of Jerusalem; A hot wind of the high hills in the wilderness toward the daughter of My people, not to fan, nor to cleanse; ¹²a wind too strong for this shall come for Me; now will I also utter judgments against them.

¹³Behold, he cometh up as clouds, and his chariots are as the whirlwind; His horses are swifter than eagles.—'Woe unto us! For we are undone.'—

¹⁵For hark! One declareth from Dan, and announceth calamity from the hills of Ephraim: ¹⁶'Make ye mention to the nations: Behold—publish concerning Jerusalem—watchers come from a far country, and give out their voice against the cities of Judah.'

¹⁷As keepers of a field are they against her round about; because

she hath been rebellious against Me, saith the Lord. [18]Thy way and thy doings have procured these things unto thee; this is thy wickedness; yea, it is bitter, yea, it reacheth unto thy heart. [19]My bowels, my bowels! I writhe in pain! The chambers of my heart! My heart moaneth within me! I cannot hold my peace! Because thou hast heard, O my soul, the sound of the horn, the alarm of war.

[20]Destruction followeth upon destruction, for the whole land is spoiled; suddenly are my tents spoiled, my curtains in a moment. [21]How long shall I see the standard, shall I hear the sound of the horn?

[22]For My people is foolish, they know Me not; they are sottish children, and they have no understanding; they are wise to do evil, but to do good they have no knowledge.

[23]I beheld the earth, and, lo, it was waste and void; and the heavens, and they had no light. [24]I beheld the mountains, and, lo, they trembled, and all the hills moved to and fro. [25]I beheld, and, lo, there was no man, and all the birds of the heavens were fled. [26]I beheld, and, lo, the fruitful field was a wilderness, and all the cities thereof were broken down at the presence of the Lord, and before His fierce anger.

[27]For thus saith the Lord: The whole land shall be desolate; yet will I not make a full end. [28]For this shall the earth mourn, and the heavens above be black; because I have spoken it, I have purposed it, and I have not repented, neither will I turn back from it.

[29]For the noise of the horsemen and bowmen the whole city fleeth; they go into the thickets, and climb up upon the rocks; every city is forsaken, and not a man dwelleth therein.

[30]And thou, that art spoiled, what doest thou, that thou clothest thyself with scarlet, that thou deckest thee with ornaments of gold, that thou enlargest thine eyes with paint? In vain dost thou make thyself fair; thy lovers despise thee, they seek thy life.

[31]For I have heard a voice as of a woman in travail, the anguish as of her that bringeth forth her first child, the voice of the daughter of Zion, that gaspeth for breath, that spreadeth her hands: 'Woe is me, now! for my soul fainteth before the murderers.'

[5:1]Run ye to and fro through the streets of Jerusalem, and see now, and know, and seek in the broad places thereof, if ye can find a man, if there be any that doeth justly, that seeketh truth; and I will pardon her. [2]And though they say: 'As the Lord liveth', surely they swear falsely.

[3]O Lord, are not Thine eyes upon truth? Thou hast stricken them, but they were not affected; Thou hast consumed them, but they have refused to receive correction; they have made their faces harder than a rock; they have refused to return.

[4]And I said: 'Surely these are poor, they are foolish, for they know not the way of the Lord, nor the ordinance of their God; [5]I will get me unto the great men, and will speak unto them; for they know the way of the Lord, and the ordinance of their God.' But these had altogether broken the yoke, and burst the bands. [6]Wherefore a lion out of the forest doth slay them, a wolf of the deserts doth spoil them, a leopard watcheth over their cities, every one that goeth out thence is torn in pieces; because their transgressions are many, their backslidings are increased.

[7]Wherefore should I pardon thee? The children have forsaken Me, and sworn by no-gods; and when I had fed them to the full, they committed adultery, and assembled themselves in troops at the harlots' houses. [8]They are become as well-fed horses, lusty stallions; every one neigheth after his neighbour's wife. [9]Shall I not punish for these things? saith the Lord; and shall not My soul be avenged on such a nation as this?

[10]Go ye up into her rows, and destroy, but make not a full end; take away her shoots; for they are not the Lord's.

[11]For the house of Israel and the house of Judah have dealt very treacherously against Me, saith the Lord. [12]They have belied the Lord, and said: 'It is not He, neither shall evil come upon us; neither shall we see sword nor famine; [13]and the prophets shall become wind, and the word is not in them; thus be it done unto them.'

[14]Wherefore thus saith the Lord, the God of hosts: Because ye speak this word, behold, I will make My words in thy mouth fire, and this people wood, and it shall devour them.

[15]Lo, I will bring a nation upon you from far, O house of Israel,

saith the Lord; It is an enduring nation, it is an ancient nation, a nation whose language thou knowest not, neither understandest what they say. [16]Their quiver is an open sepulchre, they are all mighty men. [17]And they shall eat up thy harvest, and thy bread, they shall eat up thy sons and thy daughters, they shall eat up thy flocks and thy herds, they shall eat up thy vines and thy fig-trees; they shall batter thy fortified cities, wherein thou trusteth, with the sword. [18]But even in those days, saith the Lord, I will not make a full end with you.

[19]And it shall come to pass, when ye shall say: 'Wherefore hath the Lord our God done all these things unto us?' Then shalt Thou say unto them: 'Like as ye have forsaken Me, and served strange gods in your land, so shall ye serve strangers in a land that is not yours.'

[20]Declare ye this in the house of Jacob, and announce it in Judah, saying: [21]Hear now this, O foolish people, and without understanding, that have eyes, and see not, that have ears, and hear not: [22]Fear ye not Me? saith the Lord; will ye not tremble at My presence? Who have placed the sand for the bound of the sea, an everlasting ordinance, which it cannot pass; and though the waves thereof toss themselves, yet can they not prevail; though they roar, yet can they not pass over it.

[23]But this people hath a revolting and a rebellious heart; they are revolted, and gone. [24]Neither say they in their heart: 'Let us now fear the Lord our God, that giveth the former rain, and the latter in due season; that keepeth for us the appointed weeks of the harvest.'

[25]Your iniquities have turned away these things, and your sins have withholden good from you. [26]For among My people are found wicked men; they pry, as fowlers lie in wait; they set a trap, they catch men. [27]As a cage is full of birds, so are their houses full of deceit; therefore they are become great, and waxen rich; [28]They are waxen fat, they are become sleek; yea, they overpass in deeds of wickedness; they plead not the cause, the cause of the fatherless, that they might make it to prosper; and the right of the needy do they not judge. [29]Shall I not punish for these things? saith

the Lord; shall not My soul be avenged on such a nation as this?

[30]An appalling and horrible thing Is come to pass in the land: [31]The prophets prophesy in the service of falsehood, and the priests bear rule at their beck; and My people love to have it so; what then will ye do in the end thereof?

[6:1]Put yourselves under covert, ye children of Benjamin, away from the midst of Jerusalem, and blow the horn in Tekoa, and set up a signal on Beth-cherem; for evil looketh forth from the north, and a great destruction.

[2]The comely and delicate one, the daughter of Zion, will I cut off. [3]Shepherds with their flocks come unto her; they pitch their tents against her round about; they feed bare every one what is nigh at hand. [4]'Prepare ye war against her; arise, and let us go up at noon!

'Woe unto us! for the day declineth, for the shadows of the evening are stretched out! [5]'Arise, and let us go up by night, and let us destroy her palaces.'

[6]For thus hath the Lord of hosts said: Hew ye down her trees, and cast up a mound against Jerusalem; this is the city to be punished; everywhere there is oppression in the midst of her. [7]As a cistern welleth with her waters, so she welleth with her wickedness; violence and spoil is heard in her; before Me continually is sickness and wounds.

[9]Thus saith the Lord of hosts: They shall thoroughly glean as a vine the remnant of Israel; turn again thy hand as a grape-gatherer upon the shoots. [10]to whom shall I speak and give warning, that they may hear? Behold, their ear is dull, and they cannot attend; behold, the word of the Lord is become unto them a reproach, they have no delight in it.

[11]Therefore I am full of the fury of the Lord, I am weary with holding in: pour it out upon the babes in the street, and upon the assembly of young men together; for even the husband with the wife shall be taken, the aged with him that is full of days. [12]And their houses shall be turned unto others, their fields and their wives together; for I will stretch out My hand upon the inhabitants of the land, saith the Lord.

[13]For from the least of them even unto the greatest of them

every one is greedy for gain; and from the prophet even unto the priest every one dealeth falsely. [14]They have healed also the hurt of My people lightly, saying: 'Peace, peace', when there is no peace.

[15]They shall be put to shame because they have committed abomination; yea, they are not at all ashamed, neither know they how to blush; therefore they shall fall among them that fall, at the time that I punish them they shall stumble, saith the Lord.

Prophecy of Destruction (6:16-21)

This passage from the Book of 605 is a typical prophecy of destruction that could have been made at many points in Jeremiah's career after the death of Josiah.

[6:16]Thus saith the Lord: Stand ye in the ways and see, and ask for the old paths, where is the good way, and walk therein, and ye shall find rest for your souls. But they said: 'We will not walk therein.'

[17]And I set watchmen over you: 'Attend to the sound of the horn', but they said: 'We will not attend.'

[18]Therefore hear, ye nations, and know, O congregation, what is against them. [19]Hear, O earth: behold, I will bring evil upon this people, even the fruit of their thoughts, because they have not attended unto My words, and as for My teaching, they have rejected it.

[20]To what purpose is to Me the frankincense that cometh from Sheba, and the sweet cane, from a far country? Your burnt-offerings are not acceptable, nor your sacrifices pleasing unto Me.

[21]Therefore thus saith the Lord: Behold, I will lay stumbling blocks before this people, and the fathers and the sons together shall stumble against them, the neighbour and his friend, and they shall perish.

[22]Thus saith the Lord: Behold, a people cometh from the north country, and a great nation shall be roused from the uttermost parts of the earth. [23]They lay hold on bow and spear, they are cruel, and have no compassion; their voice is like the roaring sea, and they

ride upon horses; set in array, as a man for war, against thee, O daughter of Zion.

²⁴'We have heard the fame thereof, our hands wax feeble, anguish hath taken hold of us, and pain, as of a woman in travail.'

²⁵Go not forth into the field, nor walk by the way; for there is the sword of the enemy, and terror on every side.

²⁶O daughter of my people, gird thee with sackcloth, and wallow thyself in ashes; make thee mourning, as for an only son, most bitter lamentation; for the spoiler shall suddenly come upon us.

Prophecy of Destruction (6:27-30)

This brief passage from the Book of 605 is another typical prophecy of destruction that could have been made at many points in Jeremiah's career after the death of Josiah.

⁶:²⁷I have made thee a tower and a fortress among My people; that thou mayest know and try their way. ²⁸They are all grievous revolters, going about with slanders; they are brass and iron; they all of them deal corruptly.

²⁹The bellows blow fiercely, the lead is consumed of the fire; in vain doth the founder refine, for the wicked are not separated. ³⁰Refuse silver shall men call them, because the Lord hath rejected them.

Prophecy of Destruction (7:16-19, 7:27-8:3)

This passage from the Book of 605 is interwoven with the text of the Temple Sermon.

We can see that 7:1 - 8:3 is made of two interwoven texts for the following reason: The text from 7:1 to 7:15, ending with the threat that Jerusalem will be destroyed like Shiloh if they don't obey, corresponds to the description of the Temple Sermon in 26:4-6. There is a change in 7:16-19: Jeremiah had been speaking to the people in the Temple, but at this point, God begins speaking to Jeremiah. In 7:20-26, Jeremiah is speaking to the people again, and this might be a continuation of the Temple Sermon. In 7:27-8:3, God is speaking to Jeremiah again, and the passage looks like a continuation of 7:16-19.

Thus, it seems that an editor combined the Temple Sermon with this typical prophecy of destruction that could have been made at many points in Jeremiah's career after the death of Josiah.

Some of the wording here is reminiscent of Jeremiah's prophecy at Topheth, which he gave shortly after the Temple Sermon. The prophecy at Topheth says:

> 19:5and [they] have built the high places of Baal, to burn their sons in the fire for burnt-offerings unto Baal; which I commanded not, nor spoke it, neither came it into My mind. 6Therefore, behold, the days come, saith the Lord, that this place shall no more be called Topheth, nor The valley of the son of Hinnom, but The valley of slaughter;

while this passage says:

> 7:31And they have built the high places of Topheth, which is in the valley of the son of Hinnom, to burn their sons and their daughters in the fire; which I commanded not, neither came it into My mind. 32Therefore, behold, the days come, saith the Lord, that it shall no more be called Topheth, nor The valley of the son of Hinnom, but The valley of slaughter;

Thus, parts of this passage might have originated as another version of the prophecy at Topheth, but there is not enough historical narrative here to say with certainty. .

7:16Therefore pray not thou for this people, neither lift up cry nor prayer for them, neither make intercession to Me; for I will not hear thee. 17Seest thou not what they do in the cities of Judah and in the streets of Jerusalem? 18The children gather wood, and the fathers kindle the fire, and the women knead the dough, to make cakes to the queen of heaven, and to pour out drink-offerings unto other gods, that they may provoke Me. 19Do they provoke Me?

saith the Lord; do they not provoke themselves, to the confusion of their own faces?

²⁷And thou shalt speak all these words unto them, but they will not hearken to thee; thou shalt also call unto them, but they will not answer thee. ²⁸Therefore thou shalt say unto them:

This is the nation that hath not hearkened to the voice of the Lord their God, nor received correction; Faithfulness is perished, and is cut off from their mouth.

²⁹Cut off thy hair, and cast it away, and take up a lamentation on the high hills; For the Lord hath rejected and forsaken the generation of His wrath.

³⁰For the children of Judah have done that which is evil in My sight, saith the Lord; they have set their detestable things in the house whereon My name is called, to defile it. ³¹And they have built the high places of Topheth, which is in the valley of the son of Hinnom, to burn their sons and their daughters in the fire; which I commanded not, neither came it into My mind. ³²Therefore, behold, the days come, saith the Lord, that it shall no more be called Topheth, nor The valley of the son of Hinnom, but The valley of slaughter; for they shall bury in Topheth, for lack of room. ³³And the carcasses of this people shall be food for the fowls of the heaven, and for the beasts of the earth; and none shall frighten them away. ³⁴Then will I cause to cease from the cities of Judah, and from the streets of Jerusalem, the voice of mirth and the voice of gladness, the voice of the bridegroom and the voice of the bride; for the land shall be desolate.

^{8:1}At that time, saith the Lord, they shall bring out the bones of the kings of Judah, and the bones of his princes, and the bones of the priests, and the bones of the prophets, and the bones of the inhabitants of Jerusalem, out of their graves; ²and they shall spread them before the sun, and the moon, and all the host of heaven, whom they have loved, and whom they have served, and after whom they have walked, and whom they have sought, and whom they have worshipped; they shall not be gathered, nor be buried, they shall be for dung upon the face of the earth. ³And death shall be chosen rather than life by all the residue that remain of this evil

family, that remain in all the places whither I have driven them, saith the Lord of hosts.

Prophecy of Destruction (8:4-9:15)

This passage seems to have been written at the beginning of a Babylonian invasion before Judah has retreated into its fortified cities, since it says "⁸:¹⁴Why do we sit still? Assemble yourselves, and let us enter into the fortified cities, and let us be cut off there." But there is no way of knowing whether it is the invasion that led to the first siege of Jerusalem in Jehoiakim's time or to the second siege in Zedekiah's time. Its location in the Book of 605 doesn't give us a clue, since both of these invasions came after 605; Jeremiah also might be prophesying another future invasion. Thus, this is another undateable prophecy of destruction.

Dan was the northernmost of the Israelite tribes, so when Jeremiah says "⁸:¹⁶The snorting of his horses is heard from Dan," he simply means that the invaders are coming from the north.

Notice that this passage condemns Judah for moral sins as well as for worshipping other gods: "⁹:³... every brother acteth subtly, and every neighbour goeth about with slanders. ⁴and they deceive every one his neighbour, and truth they speak not; they have taught their tongue to speak lies, they weary themselves to commit iniquity."

⁸:⁴Moreover thou shalt say unto them: Thus saith the Lord: Do men fall, and not rise up again? Doth one turn away, and not return? ⁵Why then is this people of Jerusalem slidden back by a perpetual backsliding? They hold fast deceit, they refuse to return. ⁶I attended and listened, but they spoke not aright; no man repenteth him of his wickedness, saying: 'What have I done?' Every one turneth away in his course, as a horse that rusheth headlong in the battle. ⁷Yea, the stork in the heaven knoweth her appointed times; and the turtle and the swallow and the crane observe the time of their coming; but My people know not the ordinance of the Lord.

⁸How do ye say: 'We are wise, and the Law of the Lord is with

us'? Lo, certainly in vain hath wrought the vain pen of the scribes.

⁹The wise men are ashamed, they are dismayed and taken; lo, they have rejected the word of the Lord; and what wisdom is in them? ¹⁰Therefore will I give their wives unto others, and their fields to them that shall possess them; for from the least even unto the greatest every one is greedy for gain, from the prophet even unto the priest every one dealeth falsely. ¹¹And they have healed the hurt of the daughter of My people lightly, Saying: 'Peace, peace', when there is no peace.

¹²They shall be put to shame because they have committed abomination; yea, they are not at all ashamed, neither know they how to blush; therefore shall they fall among them that fall, in the time of their visitation they shall stumble, saith the Lord. ¹³I will utterly consume them, saith the Lord; there are no grapes on the vine, nor figs on the fig-tree, and the leaf is faded; and I gave them that which they transgress.

¹⁴'Why do we sit still? Assemble yourselves, and let us enter into the fortified cities, and let us be cut off there; for the Lord our God hath cut us off, and given us water of gall to drink, because we have sinned against the Lord. ¹⁵We looked for peace, but no good came; and for a time of healing, and behold terror!'

¹⁶The snorting of his horses is heard from Dan; at the sound of the neighing of his strong ones the whole land trembleth; for they are come, and have devoured the land and all that is in it, the city and those that dwell therein. ¹⁷For, behold, I will send serpents, basilisks, among you, which will not be charmed; and they shall bite you, saith the Lord.

¹⁸Though I would take comfort against sorrow, my heart is faint within me. ¹⁹Behold the voice of the cry of the daughter of my people from a land far off: 'Is not the Lord in Zion? Is not her King in her?'—'Why have they provoked Me with their graven images, And with strange vanities?'—

²⁰'The harvest is past, the summer is ended, and we are not saved.' ²¹For the hurt of the daughter of my people am I seized with anguish; I am black, appalment hath taken hold on me. ²²Is there no balm in Gilead? Is there no physician there? Why then is

not the health of the daughter of my people recovered?

²³Oh that my head were waters, and mine eyes a fountain of tears, that I might weep day and night for the slain of the daughter of my people!

⁹:¹Oh that I were in the wilderness, in a lodging-place of wayfaring men, that I might leave my people, and go from them! For they are all adulterers, an assembly of treacherous men. ²And they bend their tongue, their bow of falsehood; and they are grown mighty in the land, but not for truth; for they proceed from evil to evil, and Me they know not, saith the Lord.

³Take ye heed every one of his neighbour, and trust ye not in any brother; for every brother acteth subtly, and every neighbour goeth about with slanders. ⁴And they deceive every one his neighbour, and truth they speak not; they have taught their tongue to speak lies, they weary themselves to commit iniquity. ⁵Thy habitation is in the midst of deceit; through deceit they refuse to know Me, Saith the Lord.

⁶Therefore thus saith the Lord of hosts: Behold, I will smelt them, and try them; for how else should I do, because of the daughter of My people? ⁷Their tongue is a sharpened arrow, it speaketh deceit; one speaketh peaceably to his neighbour with his mouth, but in his heart he layeth wait for him.

⁸Shall I not punish them for these things? saith the Lord; shall not My soul be avenged on such a nation as this?

⁹For the mountains will I take up a weeping and wailing, and for the pastures of the wilderness a lamentation, because they are burned up, so that none passeth through, and they hear not the voice of the cattle; both the fowl of the heavens and the beast are fled, and gone. ¹⁰And I will make Jerusalem heaps, a lair of jackals; and I will make the cities of Judah a desolation, without an inhabitant.

¹¹Who is the wise man, that he may understand this? And who is he to whom the mouth of the Lord hath spoken, that he may declare it? Wherefore is the land perished and laid waste like a wilderness, so that none passeth through?

¹²And the Lord saith: Because they have forsaken My law

which I set before them, and have not hearkened to My voice, neither walked therein; [13]but have walked after the stubbornness of their own heart, and after the Baalim, which their fathers taught them. [14]Therefore thus saith the Lord of hosts, the God of Israel: Behold, I will feed them, even this people, with wormwood, and give them water of gall to drink. [15]I will scatter them also among the nations, whom neither they nor their fathers have known; and I will send the sword after them, till I have consumed them.

Destruction has Occurred (9:16-21)

Rather than being a prophecy of destruction, this passage says the destruction has already occurred. Some scholars have suggested that it was written after the first Babylonian siege succeeded and some Judeans were exiled, while others have suggested that it was written after the second Babylonian siege succeeded and the mass of Judeans were exiled. It is impossible to know which, so it is classified here as undated.

It is in the Book of 605, but it must be a later addition since both of these sieges occurred after 605. Some scholars say that it is genuine, but others say it is a later text written in exilic times and attributed to Jeremiah.

[9:16]Thus saith the Lord of hosts: Consider ye, and call for the mourning women, that they may come; and send for the wise women, that they may come; [17]let them make haste, and take up a wailing for us, that our eyes may run down with tears, and our eyelids gush out with waters.

[18]For a voice of wailing is heard out of Zion: 'How are we undone! We are greatly confounded, because we have forsaken the land, because our dwellings have cast us out.'

[19]Yea, hear the word of the Lord, O ye women, and let your ear receive the word of His mouth, and teach your daughters wailing, and every one her neighbour lamentation: [20]'For death is come up into our windows, it is entered into our palaces, to cut off the children from the street, and the young men from the broad places.—

²¹Speak: Thus saith the Lord—And the carcasses of men fall as dung upon the open field, and as the handful after the harvestman, which none gathereth.'

Miscellaneous Sayings (9:22-10:16)

This collection of miscellaneous sayings is an insertion. Most or all of the sayings are not by Jeremiah.

⁹:²²Thus saith the Lord: Let not the wise man glory in his wisdom, neither let the mighty man glory in his might, let not the rich man glory in his riches; ²³but let him that glorieth glory in this, that he understandeth, and knoweth Me, that I am the Lord who exercise mercy, justice, and righteousness, in the earth; for in these things I delight, saith the Lord.

⁹:²⁴Behold, the days come, saith the Lord, that I will punish all them that are circumcised in their uncircumcision: ²⁵Egypt, and Judah, and Edom, and the children of Ammon, and Moab, and all that have the corners of their hair polled, that dwell in the wilderness; for all the nations are uncircumcised, but all the house of Israel are uncircumcised in the heart.

¹⁰:¹Hear ye the word which the Lord speaketh unto you, O house of Israel; ²thus saith the Lord: Learn not the way of the nations, and be not dismayed at the signs of heaven; for the nations are dismayed at them.

³For the customs of the peoples are vanity; for it is but a tree which one cutteth out of the forest, the work of the hands of the workman with the axe. ⁴They deck it with silver and with gold, they fasten it with nails and with hammers, that it move not. ⁵They are like a pillar in a garden of cucumbers, and speak not; they must needs be borne, because they cannot go. Be not afraid of them, for they cannot do evil, neither is it in them to do good.

⁶There is none like unto Thee, O Lord; Thou art great, and Thy name is great in might. ⁷Who would not fear Thee, O king of the

nations? For it befitteth Thee; forasmuch as among all the wise men of the nations, and in all their royalty, there is none like unto Thee.

[8]But they are altogether brutish and foolish: The vanities by which they are instructed are but a stock; [9]silver beaten into plates which is brought from Tarshish, and gold from Uphaz, the work of the craftsman and of the hands of the goldsmith; blue and purple is their clothing; they are all the work of skilful men.

[10]But the Lord God is the true God, He is the living God, and the everlasting King; at His wrath the earth trembleth, and the nations are not able to abide His indignation.

[11]Thus shall ye say unto them: 'The gods that have not made the heavens and the earth, these shall perish from the earth, and from under the heavens.' [12]He that hath made the earth by His power, that hath established the world by His wisdom, and hath stretched out the heavens by His understanding; [13]At the sound of His giving a multitude of waters in the heavens, when He causeth the vapours to ascend from the ends of the earth; when He maketh lightnings with the rain, and bringeth forth the wind out of His treasuries; [14]every man is proved to be brutish, without knowledge, every goldsmith is put to shame by the graven image, his molten image is falsehood, and there is no breath in them.

[15]They are vanity, a work of delusion; in the time of their visitation they shall perish. [16]Not like these is the portion of Jacob; for He is the former of all things, and Israel is the tribe of His inheritance; the Lord of hosts is His name.

Prophecy During a Siege (10:17-25)

This prophecy was made during a siege, judging from its first line, and it refers to the destruction of the country that occurred as the Judeans retreated into their fortified cities. It is classified here as undated because there is no way to tell whether it refers to the first Babylonian siege in the time of Jehoiakim or the second in the time of Zedekiah. It is in the Book of 605, but it must be a later insertion since both of these sieges occurred after 605.

^{10:17}Gather up thy wares from the ground, O thou that abidest in the siege. ¹⁸For thus saith the Lord: Behold, I will sling out the inhabitants of the land at this time, and will distress them, that they may feel it.

¹⁹Woe is me for my hurt! My wound is grievous; but I said: 'This is but a sickness, and I must bear it.'

²⁰My tent is spoiled, and all my cords are broken; my children are gone forth of me, and they are not; there is none to stretch forth my tent any more, and to set up my curtains. ²¹For the shepherds are become brutish, and have not inquired of the Lord; therefore they have not prospered, and all their flocks are scattered.

²²Hark! A report, behold, it cometh, and a great commotion out of the north country, to make the cities of Judah desolate, a dwelling-place of jackals.

²³O Lord, I know that man's way is not his own; it is not in man to direct his steps as he walketh. ²⁴O Lord, correct me, but in measure; not in Thine anger, lest Thou diminish me.

²⁵Pour out Thy wrath upon the nations that know Thee not, and upon the families that call not on Thy name; for they have devoured Jacob, yea, they have devoured him and consumed him, and have laid waste his habitation.

Prophecy of Destruction (11:1-17)

This is another of those typical prophecies of destruction that Jeremiah could have made at many times after the death of Josiah.

There are some hints that could date it shortly after the death of Josiah. "^{11:10}They are turned back to the iniquities of their forefathers" sounds like it might have come shortly after the reform was abandoned. Prophecies of the destruction of both Israel and Judah (11:10, 17) sounds like they might have come shortly after he was prophesying the redemption of Israel as well as Judah during the reform. But these hints are not enough to date the passage with certainty.

^{11:1}The word that came to Jeremiah from the Lord, saying: ²'Hear ye the words of this covenant, and speak unto the men of Judah,

and to the inhabitants of Jerusalem; [3]and say thou unto them: Thus saith the Lord, the God of Israel: Cursed be the man that heareth not the words of this covenant, [4]which I commanded your fathers in the day that I brought them forth out of the land of Egypt, out of the iron furnace, saying: Hearken to My voice, and do them, according to all which I command you; so shall ye be My people, and I will be your God; [5]that I may establish the oath which I swore unto your fathers, to give them a land flowing with milk and honey, as at this day.' Then answered I, and said: 'Amen, O Lord.'

[6]And the Lord said unto me: 'Proclaim all these words in the cities of Judah, and in the streets of Jerusalem, saying: Hear ye the words of this covenant, and do them. [7]For I earnestly forewarned your fathers in the day that I brought them up out of the land of Egypt, even unto this day, forewarning betimes and often, saying: Hearken to My voice. [8]Yet they hearkened not, nor inclined their ear, but walked every one in the stubbornness of their evil heart; therefore I brought upon them all the words of this covenant, which I commanded them to do, but they did them not.'

[9]And the Lord said unto me: 'A conspiracy is found among the men of Judah, and among the inhabitants of Jerusalem. [10]They are turned back to the iniquities of their forefathers, who refused to hear My words; and they are gone after other gods to serve them; the house of Israel and the house of Judah have broken My covenant which I made with their fathers. [11]Therefore thus saith the Lord: Behold, I will bring evil upon them, which they shall not be able to escape; and though they shall cry unto Me, I will not hearken unto them. [12]Then shall the cities of Judah and the inhabitants of Jerusalem go and cry unto the gods unto whom they offer; but they shall not save them at all in the time of their trouble. [13]For according to the number of thy cities are thy gods, O Judah; and according to the number of the streets of Jerusalem have ye set up altars to the shameful thing, even altars to offer unto Baal. [14]Therefore pray not thou for this people, neither lift up cry nor prayer for them; for I will not hear them in the time that they cry unto Me for their trouble.'

[15]What hath My beloved to do in My house, seeing she hath

wrought lewdness with many, and the hallowed flesh is passed from thee? When thou doest evil, then thou rejoicest.

[16]The Lord called thy name a leafy olive-tree, fair with goodly fruit; with the noise of a great tumult He hath kindled fire upon it, and the branches of it are broken.

[17]For the Lord of hosts, that planted thee, hath pronounced evil against thee, because of the evil of the house of Israel and of the house of Judah, which they have wrought for themselves in provoking Me by offering unto Baal.

Threat to Jeremiah's Life (11:18-23)

This passage is about the men of Anathoth threatening to kill Jeremiah who was himself one of the priests of Anathoth (1:1). It would be very interesting to know when other men of Anathoth threatened him to prevent him from prophesying (11:21) and then conspired to kill him (11:19), but unfortunately, this passages contain all we know about this plot against Jeremiah, and there is not enough information to date it.

We obviously have only fragments of a longer text, since the passage begins with "[11:18]And the Lord gave me knowledge of it, and I knew it; then Thou showedst me their doings" without any previous mention of what it is that Jeremiah knew about. This comes after a passage about a conspiracy of the men of Judah to turn back to the sins of their fathers (11:9), which is clearly different from the conspiracy to kill Jeremiah, though the editor who combined the texts seems to have conflated them.

Some scholars suggest that this happened early in Jeremiah's career, during the reign of Josiah, but Jeremiah had not made much of a public impression at that time. It is more likely that the men of Anathoth wanted to silence Jeremiah when he was very controversial, during the reign of Jehoiakim or Zedekiah, perhaps because his defiance was turning the king against all the other priests of Anathoth as well as against Jeremiah.

The plot described in these passages may possibly be the same plot described in 18:18-23.

¹¹:¹⁸And the Lord gave me knowledge of it, and I knew it; then Thou showedst me their doings.

¹⁹But I was like a docile lamb that is led to the slaughter; and I knew not that they had devised devices against me: 'Let us destroy the tree with the fruit thereof, and let us cut him off from the land of the living, that his name may be no more remembered.'

²⁰But, O Lord of hosts, that judgest righteously, that triest the reins and the heart, let me see Thy vengeance on them; for unto Thee have I revealed my cause.

²¹Therefore thus saith the Lord concerning the men of Anathoth, that seek thy life, saying: 'Thou shalt not prophesy in the name of the Lord, that thou die not by our hand'; ²²therefore thus saith the Lord of hosts: Behold, I will punish them; the young men shall die by the sword, their sons and their daughters shall die by famine; ²³and there shall be no remnant unto them; for I will bring evil upon the men of Anathoth, even the year of their visitation.

Miscellaneous Sayings (12:1-12:6)

This is a collection of several brief sayings. The call for vengeance (12:3) and the statement that Jeremiah's brethren have been treacherous to him (12:6) have some plausible connection with the plot against Jeremiah's life, and that is probably why an early editor located this passage right after the story of that plot.

¹²:¹Right wouldest Thou be, O Lord, were I to contend with Thee, yet will I reason with Thee: Wherefore doth the way of the wicked prosper? Wherefore are all they secure that deal very treacherously?

²Thou hast planted them, yea, they have taken root; they grow, yea, they bring forth fruit; Thou art near in their mouth, and far from their reins.

³But Thou, O Lord, knowest me, Thou seest me, and triest my heart toward Thee; pull them out like sheep for the slaughter, and prepare them for the day of slaughter.

¹²:⁴How long shall the land mourn, and the herbs of the whole field

wither? For the wickedness of them that dwell therein, the beasts are consumed, and the birds; because they said: 'He seeth not our end.'

⁵'If thou hast run with the footmen, and they have wearied thee, then how canst thou contend with horses? And though in a land of peace thou art secure, yet how wilt thou do in the thickets of the Jordan?

⁶For even thy brethren, and the house of thy father, even they have dealt treacherously with thee, even they have cried aloud after thee; believe them not, though they speak fair words unto thee.'

Destruction has Occurred (12:7-13)

Here, the destruction seems to have already occurred rather than being prophesied for the future. Thus, this passage may date from the exile at the end of Jehoiachin's reign or from the exile at the end of Zedekiah's reign.

There is a double meaning in 12:9 that is lost in translation: the Hebrew word translated as "speckled" can also mean "hypocritical."

¹²:⁷I have forsaken My house, I have cast off My heritage; I have given the dearly beloved of My soul Into the hand of her enemies.

⁸My heritage is become unto Me As a lion in the forest; She hath uttered her voice against Me; therefore have I hated her.

⁹Is My heritage unto Me as a speckled bird of prey? Are the birds of prey against her round about? Come ye, assemble all the beasts of the field, bring them to devour.

¹⁰Many shepherds have destroyed My vineyard, they have trodden My portion under foot, they have made My pleasant portion a desolate wilderness. ¹¹They have made it a desolation, it mourneth unto Me, being desolate; the whole land is made desolate, because no man layeth it to heart.

¹²Upon all the high hills in the wilderness spoilers are come; for the sword of the Lord devoureth from the one end of the land even to the other end of the land, no flesh hath peace.

¹³They have sown wheat, and have reaped thorns; they have put themselves to pain, they profit not; be ye then ashamed of your increase, because of the fierce anger of the Lord.

I Will Bring Them Back (12:14-17)

This seems to be an exilic passage written after Jeremiah's death. Israel and Judah have already been exiled, and their lands have been occupied by "evil neighbours," but if they repent, they will be able to return to their lands.

¹²:¹⁴Thus saith the Lord: As for all Mine evil neighbours, that touch the inheritance which I have caused My people Israel to inherit, behold, I will pluck them up from off their land, and will pluck up the house of Judah from among them. ¹⁵And it shall come to pass, after that I have plucked them up, I will again have compassion on them; and I will bring them back, every man to his heritage, and every man to his land. ¹⁶And it shall come to pass, if they will diligently learn the ways of My people to swear by My name: 'As the Lord liveth, 'even as they taught My people to swear by Baal; then shall they be built up in the midst of My people. ¹⁷But if they will not hearken, then will I pluck up that nation, plucking up and destroying it, saith the Lord.

Prophecies of Destruction (13:1-17)

Here again we have typical prophecies of destruction that could have come at many times in Jeremiah's career after the death of Josiah. Verses 13:15-17 call for repentance to avoid destruction, which is not typical of this late period; these verses might be from early in Jeremiah's career, but they cannot be dated with confidence.

¹³:¹Thus said the Lord unto me: 'Go, and get thee a linen girdle, and put it upon thy loins, and put it not in water.' ²So I got a girdle

according to the word of the Lord, and put it upon my loins.

³And the word of the Lord came unto me the second time, saying: ⁴'Take the girdle that thou hast gotten, which is upon thy loins, and arise, go to Perath, and hide it there in a cleft of the rock.' ⁵So I went, and hid it in Perath, as the Lord commanded me. ⁶And it came to pass after many days, that the Lord said unto me: 'Arise, go to Perath, and take the girdle from thence, which I commanded thee to hide there.' ⁷Then I went to Perath, and digged, and took the girdle from the place where I had hid it; and, behold, the girdle was marred, it was profitable for nothing.

⁸Then the word of the Lord came unto me, saying: ⁹Thus saith the Lord: After this manner will I mar the pride of Judah, and the great pride of Jerusalem, ¹⁰even this evil people, that refuse to hear My words, that walk in the stubbornness of their heart, and are gone after other gods to serve them, and to worship them, that it be as this girdle, which is profitable for nothing. ¹¹For as the girdle cleaveth to the loins of a man, so have I caused to cleave unto Me the whole house of Israel and the whole house of Judah, saith the Lord, that they might be unto Me for a people, and for a name, and for a praise, and for a glory; but they would not hearken.

¹²Moreover thou shalt speak unto them this word: Thus saith the Lord, the God of Israel: 'Every bottle is filled with wine'; and when they shall say unto thee: 'Do we not know that every bottle is filled with wine?' ¹³Then shalt thou say unto them: Thus saith the Lord: Behold, I will fill all the inhabitants of this land, even the kings that sit upon David's throne, and the priests, and the prophets, and all the inhabitants of Jerusalem, with drunkenness. ¹⁴And I will dash them one against another, even the fathers and the sons together, saith the Lord; I will not pity, nor spare, nor have compassion, that I should not destroy them.

¹⁵Hear ye, and give ear, be not proud; For the Lord hath spoken.

¹⁶Give glory to the Lord your God, before it grow dark, and before your feet stumble upon the mountains of twilight, and, while ye look for light, He turn it into the shadow of death, And make it gross darkness.

¹⁷But if ye will not hear it, My soul shall weep in secret for

your pride; and mine eyes shall weep sore, and run down with tears, because the Lord's flock is carried away captive.

Prophecy of Destruction (14:10-18, 15:1-4)

Jeremiah 14:1 to 15:4 clearly was created by interweaving two different texts. Verses 14:1-9 say that Judah is threatened by drought, and Jeremiah prays that God will save Judah. Verses 14:10-18 talk about destruction by sword and famine, and God tells Jeremiah not to pray for Judah because it will be destroyed. Verses 14:19-22 go back to Jeremiah praying that Judah should be saved from drought. Verses 15:1-4 go back to Judah being destroyed by sword and famine and God saying that prayers will not help.

It seems that verses 14:1-9 and 19-22 come from early in Jeremiah's career, before Josiah's reform began, because the drought is also mentioned in this early passage: "³:²... thou hast polluted the land With thy harlotries and with thy wickedness. ³Therefore the showers have been withheld, and there hath been no latter rain."

The two texts were probably interwoven by a later editor who wanted to make the earlier text more like Jeremiah's usual prophesies of destruction, but conceivably, they might have been interwoven by Jeremiah himself when he wrote the book of 605. Jeremiah tells us that God commanded him in 605 to write down all of his prophecies, and he might have obeyed by including this early prophecy but combining it with a later prophecy to bring it closer to his mood at the time, when he had begun to prophesy inevitable destruction.

The earlier text has been moved to the historical section about Josiah's reign. The balance of the combined passage is here because it cannot be dated.

It includes a couple of puzzling clues about its date. "¹⁵:¹⁸If I go forth into the field, then behold the slain with the sword! And if I enter into the city, then behold them that are sick with famine!" sounds like it was written during one of the two sieges of Jerusalem. But "*[15:4]And I will cause them to be a horror among all the kingdoms of the earth, because of Manasseh the son of Hezekiah king of Judah, for that which he did in Jerusalem" sounds much earlier. Rather than focusing on Josiah's reforms, it talks about King Manasseh, who abandoned the reforms of Josiah's great grandfather Hezekiah, and we would expect Jeremiah to be preoccupied with this earlier failure before Josiah's reform began.*

[15:10]Thus saith the Lord unto this people: Even so have they loved to wander, they have not refrained their feet; therefore the Lord doth not accept them, now will He remember their iniquity, and punish their sins.

[11]And the Lord said unto me: 'Pray not for this people for their good. [12]When they fast, I will not hear their cry; and when they offer burnt-offering and meal-offering, I will not accept them; but I will consume them by the sword, and by the famine, and by the pestilence.'

[13]Then said I: 'Ah, Lord God! Behold, the prophets say unto them: Ye shall not see the sword, neither shall ye have famine; but I will give you assured peace in this place.'

[14]Then the Lord said unto me: 'The prophets prophesy lies in My name; I sent them not, neither have I commanded them, neither spoke I unto them; they prophesy unto you a lying vision, and divination, and a thing of nought, and the deceit of their own heart. [15]Therefore thus saith the Lord: As for the prophets that prophesy in My name, and I sent them not, yet they say: Sword and famine shall not be in this land, by sword and famine shall those prophets be consumed; [16]and the people to whom they prophesy shall be cast out in the streets of Jerusalem because of the famine and the sword; and they shall have none to bury them, them, their wives, nor their sons, nor their daughters; for I will pour their evil upon them.'

[17]And thou shalt say this word unto them: Let mine eyes run down with tears night and day, and let them not cease; for the virgin daughter of my people is broken with a great breach, with a very grievous blow.

[18]If I go forth into the field, then behold the slain with the sword! And if I enter into the city, then behold them that are sick

with famine! For both the prophet and the priest are gone about to a land, and knew it not.

¹⁵:¹Then said the Lord unto me: 'Though Moses and Samuel stood before Me, yet My mind could not be toward this people; cast them out of My sight, and let them go forth. ²And it shall come to pass, when they say unto thee: Whither shall we go forth? then thou shall tell them: Thus saith the Lord: Such as are for death, to death; and such as are for the sword, to the sword; and such as are for the famine, to the famine; and such as are for captivity, to captivity. ³And I will appoint over them four kinds, saith the Lord: the sword to slay, and the dogs to drag, and the fowls of the heaven, and the beasts of the earth, to devour and to destroy. ⁴And I will cause them to be a horror among all the kingdoms of the earth, because of Manasseh the son of Hezekiah king of Judah, for that which he did in Jerusalem.

Prophecy of Destruction (16:1-13)

This is another prophecy of destruction that could have come at many times after the death of Josiah.

¹⁶:¹The word of the Lord came also unto me, saying: ²Thou shalt not take thee a wife, neither shalt thou have sons or daughters in this place.

³For thus saith the Lord concerning the sons and concerning the daughters that are born in this place, and concerning their mothers that bore them, and concerning their fathers that begot them in this land: ⁴They shall die of grievous deaths; they shall not be lamented, neither shall they be buried, they shall be as dung upon the face of the ground; and they shall be consumed by the sword, and by famine; and their carcasses shall be meat for the fowls of heaven, and for the beasts of the earth.

⁵For thus saith the Lord: Enter not into the house of mourning, neither go to lament, neither bemoan them; for I have taken away My peace from this people, saith the Lord, even mercy and compassion. ⁶Both the great and the small shall die in this land;

they shall not be buried; neither shall men lament for them, nor cut themselves, nor make themselves bald for them; [7]neither shall men break bread for them in mourning, to comfort them for the dead; neither shall men give them the cup of consolation to drink for their father or for their mother. [8]And thou shalt not go into the house of feasting to sit with them, to eat and to drink.

[9]For thus saith the Lord of hosts, the God of Israel: Behold, I will cause to cease out of this place, before your eyes and in your days, the voice of mirth and the voice of gladness, the voice of the bridegroom and the voice of the bride.

[10]And it shall come to pass, when thou shalt tell this people all these words, and they shall say unto thee: 'Wherefore hath the Lord pronounced all this great evil against us? or what is our iniquity? or what is our sin that we have committed against the Lord our God?' [11]then shalt thou say unto them: 'Because your fathers have forsaken Me, saith the Lord, and have walked after other gods, and have served them, and have worshipped them, and have forsaken Me, and have not kept My law; [12]and ye have done worse than your fathers; for, behold, ye walk every one after the stubbornness of his evil heart, so that ye hearken not unto Me; [13]therefore will I cast you out of this land into a land that ye have not known, neither ye nor your fathers; and there shall ye serve other gods day and night; forasmuch as I will show you no favour.'

Miscellaneous Sayings (16:14-18)

This is collection of brief sayings. The prophecy of return (16:14-15) and the Messianic prophecy 16:19-21) are clearly later works that were written during the Babylonian exile when Jews began to believe that a Messiah would bring them back from exile. The other prophecy might be by Jeremiah but is not dateable.

[16:14]Therefore, behold, the days come, saith the Lord, that it shall no more be said: 'As the Lord liveth, that brought up the children of Israel out of the land of Egypt,' '[15]but: 'As the Lord liveth, that brought up the children of Israel from the land of the north, and from all the countries whither He had driven them'; and I will bring them back into their land that I gave unto their fathers.

[16]Behold, I will send for many fishers, saith the Lord, and they shall fish them; and afterward I will send for many hunters, and they shall hunt them from every mountain, and from every hill, and out of the clefts of the rocks.
[17]For Mine eyes are upon all their ways, they are not hid from My face; neither is their iniquity concealed from Mine eyes. [18]And first I will recompense their iniquity and their sin double; because they have profaned My land; they have filled Mine inheritance with the carcasses of their detestable things and their abominations.

[19]O Lord, my strength, and my stronghold, and my refuge, in the day of affliction, unto Thee shall the nations come from the ends of the earth, and shall say: 'Our fathers have inherited nought but lies, vanity and things wherein there is no profit.'
[20]Shall a man make unto himself gods, and they are no gods?
[21]Therefore, behold, I will cause them to know, this once will I cause them to know My hand and My might; and they shall know that My name is the Lord.

Prophecy of Destruction of Jerusalem (15:5-9)

Because it is specifically about the destruction of Jerusalem, this passage was probably written during one of the sieges of Jerusalem, but there is no way to tell whether it was written during the first or second Babylonian siege.

[15:5]For who shall have pity upon thee, O Jerusalem? Or who shall bemoan thee? Or who shall turn aside to ask of thy welfare?
[6]Thou hast cast Me off, saith the Lord, thou art gone backward; therefore do I stretch out My hand against thee, and destroy thee; I am weary with repenting. [7]And I fan them with a fan in the gates of the land; I bereave them of children, I destroy My people, since they return not from their ways.
[8]Their widows are increased to Me above the sand of the seas;

I bring upon them, against the mother, a chosen one, even a spoiler at noonday; I cause anguish and terrors to fall upon her suddenly.

⁹She that hath borne seven languisheth; her spirit droopeth; her sun is gone down while it was yet day, she is ashamed and confounded; and the residue of them will I deliver to the sword before their enemies, saith the Lord.'

Woe Is Me (15:10-20)

Jeremiah despairs because he is persecuted here in 15:10-20 and also in 17:14-18. Jeremiah was persecuted during the reigns of Jehoiakim and Zedekiah, and we can only speculate about which episode in Jeremiah's life caused him to despair.

¹⁵:¹⁰Woe is me, my mother, that thou hast borne me a man of strife and a man of contention to the whole earth! I have not lent, neither have men lent to me; yet every one of them doth curse me.

¹¹The Lord said: 'Verily I will release thee for good; verily I will cause the enemy to make supplication unto thee in the time of evil and in the time of affliction. ¹²Can iron break iron from the north and brass? ¹³Thy substance and thy treasures will I give for a spoil without price, and that for all thy sins, even in all thy borders. ¹⁴And I will make thee to pass with thine enemies into a land which thou knowest not; for a fire is kindled in My nostril, which shall burn upon you.'

¹⁵Thou, O Lord, knowest; remember me, and think of me, and avenge me of my persecutors; take me not away because of Thy long-suffering; know that for Thy sake I have suffered taunts.

¹⁶Thy words were found, and I did eat them; and Thy words were unto me a joy and the rejoicing of my heart; because Thy name was called on me, O Lord God of hosts. ¹⁷I sat not in the assembly of them that make merry, nor rejoiced; I sat alone because of Thy hand; for Thou hast filled me with indignation.

¹⁸Why is my pain perpetual, and my wound incurable, so that it refuseth to be healed? Wilt Thou indeed be unto me as a deceitful brook, as waters that fail?

¹⁹Therefore thus saith the Lord: If thou return, and I bring thee back, thou shalt stand before Me; and if thou bring forth the precious out of the vile, thou shalt be as My mouth; let them return unto thee, but thou shalt not return unto them.

²⁰And I will make thee unto this people a fortified brazen wall; and they shall fight against thee, but they shall not prevail against thee; for I am with thee to save thee and to deliver thee, Saith the Lord. ²¹And I will deliver thee out of the hand of the wicked, and I will redeem thee out of the hand of the terrible.

Miscellaneous Sayings (17:1-13)

This is a collection of brief sayings that cannot be dated.

¹⁷:¹The sin of Judah is written with a pen of iron, and with the point of a diamond; it is graven upon the tablet of their heart, and upon the horns of your altars.

²Like the symbols of their sons are their altars, and their Asherim are by the leafy trees, upon the high hills.

³O thou that sittest upon the mountain in the field, I will give thy substance and all thy treasures for a spoil, and thy high places, because of sin, throughout all thy borders. ⁴And thou, even of thyself, shalt discontinue from thy heritage that I gave thee; and I will cause thee to serve thine enemies In the land which thou knowest not; for ye have kindled a fire in My nostril, which shall burn for ever.

⁵Thus saith the Lord: Cursed is the man that trusteth in man, and maketh flesh his arm, and whose heart departeth from the Lord. ⁶For he shall be like a tamarisk in the desert, and shall not see when good cometh; but shall inhabit the parched places in the wilderness, a salt land and not inhabited.

⁷Blessed is the man that trusteth in the Lord, and whose trust the Lord is. ⁸For he shall be as a tree planted by the waters, and that spreadeth out its roots by the river, and shall not see when heat cometh, but its foliage shall be luxuriant; and shall not be anxious

in the year of drought, neither shall cease from yielding fruit.

⁹The heart is deceitful above all things, and it is exceeding weak—who can know it?

¹⁰I the Lord search the heart, I try the reins, even to give every man according to his ways, according to the fruit of his doings.

¹¹As the partridge that broodeth over young which she hath not brought forth, so is he that getteth riches, and not by right; in the midst of his days he shall leave them, and at his end he shall be a fool.

¹²Thou throne of glory, on high from the beginning, Thou place of our sanctuary, ¹³Thou hope of Israel, the Lord! All that forsake Thee shall be ashamed; they that depart from Thee shall be written in the earth, because they have forsaken the Lord, the fountain of living waters.

Those Who Persecute Me (17:14-18)

This condemnation of those who persecute him cannot be dated. It may conceivable be connected with the plot (or plots) against Jeremiah's life in 11:21-12:6 and 18:18-23. Or it could be connected to other times in his life when Jeremiah was persecuted, such as when Zedekiah put him in prison.

¹⁷:¹⁴Heal me, O Lord, and I shall be healed; save me, and I shall be saved; for Thou art my praise. ¹⁵Behold, they say unto me: 'Where is the word of the Lord? Let it come now.'

¹⁶As for me, I have not hastened from being a shepherd after Thee; neither have I desired the woeful day; thou knowest it; that which came out of my lips was manifest before Thee.

¹⁷Be not a ruin unto me; Thou art my refuge in the day of evil. ¹⁸Let them be ashamed that persecute me, but let not me be ashamed; let them be dismayed, but let not me be dismayed; bring upon them the day of evil, and destroy them with double destruction.

Observe the Sabbath (17:19-27)

This passage is probably not authentic. This is the only place where Jeremiah calls for Sabbath observance, and it is plausible that someone who wanted to promote Sabbath observance wrote this and attributed it to Jeremiah. Parts of 17:25 are similar to "22:4For if ye do this thing indeed, then shall there enter in by the gates of this house kings sitting upon the throne of David, riding in chariots and on horses, he, and his servants, and his people."

17:19Thus said the Lord unto me: Go, and stand in the gate of the children of the people, whereby the kings of Judah come in, and by which they go out, and in all the gates of Jerusalem; 20and say unto them:

Hear ye the word of the Lord, ye kings of Judah, and all Judah, and all the inhabitants of Jerusalem, that enter in by these gates; 21thus saith the Lord: Take heed for the sake of your souls, and bear no burden on the Sabbath day, nor bring it in by the gates of Jerusalem; 22neither carry forth a burden out of your houses on the Sabbath day, neither do ye any work; but hallow ye the Sabbath day, as I commanded your fathers; 23but they hearkened not, neither inclined their ear, but made their neck stiff, that they might not hear, nor receive instruction.

24And it shall come to pass, if ye diligently hearken unto Me, saith the Lord, to bring in no burden through the gates of this city on the Sabbath day, but to hallow the Sabbath day, to do no work therein; 25then shall there enter in by the gates of this city kings and princes sitting upon the throne of David, riding in chariots and on horses, they, and their princes, the men of Judah, and the inhabitants of Jerusalem; and this city shall be inhabited for ever. 26And they shall come from the cities of Judah, and from the places round about Jerusalem, and from the land of Benjamin, and from the Lowland, and from the mountains, and from the South, bringing burnt-offerings, and sacrifices, and meal-offerings, and frankincense, and bringing sacrifices of thanksgiving, unto the house of the Lord.

27But if ye will not hearken unto Me to hallow the Sabbath

day, and not to bear a burden and enter in at the gates of Jerusalem on the Sabbath day; then will I kindle a fire in the gates thereof, and it shall devour the palaces of Jerusalem, and it shall not be quenched.

Prophecy of Destruction (18:1-12)

This seems to have been written some time after Jeremiah lost hope that Judah would repent. It calls for repentance, but it ends, "18:12But they say: There is no hope; but we will walk after our own devices, and we will do every one after the stubbornness of his evil heart."

18:1The word which came to Jeremiah from the Lord, saying: 2'Arise, and go down to the potter's house, and there I will cause thee to hear My words.' 3Then I went down to the potter's house, and, behold, he was at his work on the wheels. 4And whensoever the vessel that he made of the clay was marred in the hand of the potter, he made it again another vessel, as seemed good to the potter to make it.

5Then the word of the Lord came to me, saying: 6'O house of Israel, cannot I do with you as this potter? saith the Lord. Behold, as the clay in the potter's hand, so are ye in My hand, O house of Israel. 7At one instant I may speak concerning a nation, and concerning a kingdom, to pluck up and to break down and to destroy it; 8but if that nation turn from their evil, because of which I have spoken against it, I repent of the evil that I thought to do unto it. 9And at one instant I may speak concerning a nation, and concerning a kingdom, to build and to plant it; 10but if it do evil in My sight, that it hearken not to My voice, then I repent of the good, wherewith I said I would benefit it.

11Now therefore do thou speak to the men of Judah, and to the inhabitants of Jerusalem, saying: Thus saith the Lord: Behold, I frame evil against you, and devise a device against you; return ye now every one from his evil way, and amend your ways and your doings. 12But they say: There is no hope; but we will walk after our own devices, and we will do every one after the stubbornness of his evil heart.'

Prophecy of Destruction (18:13-17)

This is another of those prophecies of destruction that could have come at many points in Jeremiah's career after the death of Josiah.

¹⁸:¹³Therefore thus saith the Lord: Ask ye now among the nations, who hath heard such things; the virgin of Israel hath done a very horrible thing.

¹⁴Doth the snow of Lebanon fail from the rock of the field? Or are the strange cold flowing waters plucked up?

¹⁵For My people hath forgotten Me, they offer unto vanity; and they have been made to stumble in their ways, in the ancient paths, to walk in bypaths, in a way not cast up; ¹⁶to make their land an astonishment, and a perpetual hissing; every one that passeth thereby shall be astonished, and shake his head. ¹⁷I will scatter them as with an east wind before the enemy; I will look upon their back, and not their face, in the day of their calamity.

Plot Against Jeremiah (18:18-23)

The plot against Jeremiah described here may be the same plot described in 11:21-12:6 or may be an entirely different plot. Here, too, we only have a fragment of the story of the plot, so we know little about it and cannot date it with any certainty.

It begins with a conspiracy to speak against Jeremiah (18:18). Later the conspiracy becomes more serious: "¹⁸:²²... For they have digged a pit to take me, and hid snares for my feet. ²³Yet, Lord, Thou knowest all their counsel against me to slay me...." The pit and snares are obviously metaphorical, just meaning that wanted to trap him, and conceivably the counsel to slay Jeremiah might also be metaphorical, just meaning that wanted to harm him and end his career.

[18:18]Then said they: 'Come, and let us devise devices against Jeremiah; for instruction shall not perish from the priest, nor counsel from the wise, nor the word from the prophet. Come, and let us smite him with the tongue, and let us not give heed to any of his words.'

[19]Give heed to me, O Lord, and hearken to the voice of them that contend with me. [20]Shall evil be recompensed for good? For they have digged a pit for my soul. Remember how I stood before Thee to speak good for them, to turn away Thy wrath from them.

[21]Therefore deliver up their children to the famine, and hurl them to the power of the sword; and let their wives be bereaved of their children, and widows; and let their men be slain of death, and their young men smitten of the sword in battle. [22]Let a cry be heard from their houses, when Thou shalt bring a troop suddenly upon them; for they have digged a pit to take me, and hid snares for my feet.

[23]Yet, Lord, Thou knowest all their counsel against me to slay me; forgive not their iniquity, neither blot out their sin from Thy sight; but let them be made to stumble before Thee; deal Thou with them in the time of Thine anger.

Cursed Be the Day I Was Born (20:7-18)

Jeremiah despairs because he is persecuted both in this passage and in 15:10-20. We can only speculate about which episode or episodes in Jeremiah's life caused him to despair.

In the conventional text, this passage follows the sermons in Topheth and Jerusalem (19:1 - 20:6), when Pashur puts Jeremiah in the stocks. But it is not a continuation of that story, because in 20:7 he suddenly begins talking to the Lord in a way that he clearly would not do in the presence of Pashur. It seems more likely to be from later in Jeremiah's life, when he is persecuted much more harshly. It was probably placed after the episode with Pashur because is includes the verse "[20:10]For I have heard the whispering of many, Terror on every side," and in the story of Pashur, Jeremiah says "[20:3]The Lord hath not called thy name

Pashhur, but Magormissabib," which means "terror on every side."

20:7O Lord, Thou hast enticed me, and I was enticed, Thou hast overcome me, and hast prevailed; I am become a laughing-stock all the day, every one mocketh me. 8For as often as I speak, I cry out, I cry: 'Violence and spoil'; because the word of the Lord is made a reproach unto me, and a derision, all the day.

9And if I say: 'I will not make mention of Him, nor speak any more in His name', then there is in my heart as it were a burning fire shut up in my bones, and I weary myself to hold it in, but cannot. 10For I have heard the whispering of many, terror on every side: 'Denounce, and we will denounce him'; even of all my familiar friends, them that watch for my halting: 'Peradventure he will be enticed, and we shall prevail against him, and we shall take our revenge on him.'

11But the Lord is with me as a mighty warrior; therefore my persecutors shall stumble, and they shall not prevail; they shall be greatly ashamed, because they have not prospered, even with an everlasting confusion which shall never be forgotten. 12But, O Lord of hosts, that triest the righteous, that seest the reins and the heart, let me see Thy vengeance on them; for unto Thee have I revealed my cause.

13Sing unto the Lord, praise ye the Lord; for He hath delivered the soul of the needy from the hand of evil-doers.

14Cursed be the day wherein I was born; the day wherein my mother bore me, let it not be blessed.

15Cursed be the man who brought tidings to my father, saying: 'A man-child is born unto thee'; making him very glad. 16And let that man be as the cities which the Lord overthrew, and repented not; and let him hear a cry in the morning, and an alarm at noontide;

17Because he slew me not from the womb; and so my mother would have been my grave, and her womb always great.

18Wherefore came I forth out of the womb to see labour and sorrow, that my days should be consumed in shame?

Prophecy of Destruction (21:11-14, 22:1-8)

This is another prophecy of destruction that could come from many times in Jeremiah's life. It may be patched together from a number of source texts. Parts of it sound Messianic (22:4), indicating that they may have been written or at least revised during the exile and attributed to Jeremiah. Notice that this prophecy demands moral behavior to avoid judgment (21:12, 22:3) and not just religious reform.

²¹:¹¹And unto the house of the king of Judah: hear ye the word of the Lord;

¹²O house of David, thus saith the Lord: execute justice in the morning, and deliver the spoiled out of the hand of the oppressor, lest My fury go forth like fire, and burn that none can quench it, because of the evil of your doings.

¹³Behold, I am against thee, O inhabitant of the valley, and rock of the plain, saith the Lord; ye that say: 'Who shall come down against us? Or who shall enter into our habitations?' ¹⁴And I will punish you according to the fruit of your doings, saith the Lord; and I will kindle a fire in her forest, and it shall devour all that is round about her.

²²:¹Thus said the Lord: Go down to the house of the king of Judah, and speak there this word, ²and say: Hear the word of the Lord, O king of Judah, that sittest upon the throne of David, thou, and thy servants, and thy people that enter in by these gates. ³Thus saith the Lord: Execute ye justice and righteousness, and deliver the spoiled out of the hand of the oppressor; and do no wrong, do no violence, to the stranger, the fatherless, nor the widow, neither shed innocent blood in this place. ⁴For if ye do this thing indeed, then shall there enter in by the gates of this house kings sitting upon the throne of David, riding in chariots and on horses, he, and his servants, and his people. ⁵But if ye will not hear these words, I swear by Myself, saith the Lord, that this house shall become a desolation.

⁶For thus saith the Lord concerning the house of the king of Judah: Thou art Gilead unto Me, the head of Lebanon; yet surely I

will make thee a wilderness, cities which are not inhabited. [7]And I will prepare destroyers against thee, every one with his weapons; and they shall cut down thy choice cedars, and cast them into the fire.

[8]And many nations shall pass by this city, and they shall say every man to his neighbour: 'Wherefore hath the Lord done thus unto this great city?' [9]Then they shall answer: 'Because they forsook the covenant of the Lord their God, and worshipped other gods, and served them.'

Lamentation (22:20-23)

This brief lamentation apparently is from a time when Jerusalem fell to the Babylonians and was about to be sent into captivity, but there is not context to let us guess whether it was the fall of Jerusalem under Jehoiachin or under Zedekiah.

[22:20]Go up to Lebanon, and cry, and lift up thy voice in Bashan; and cry from Abarim, for all thy lovers are destroyed.

[21]I spoke unto thee in thy prosperity, but thou saidst: 'I will not hear.' This hath been thy manner from thy youth, that thou hearkenedst not to My voice.

[22]The wind shall feed upon all thy shepherds, and thy lovers shall go into captivity; surely then shalt thou be ashamed and confounded for all thy wickedness.

[23]O inhabitant of Lebanon, that art nestled in the cedars, how gracious shalt thou be when pangs come upon thee, the pain as of a woman in travail!

Messianic Prophecy (23:1-8)

This passage, near the end of the Book of 605, is clearly a later text that was attributed to Jeremiah. The messianic prediction that Israel will return from Babylon and will be ruled by a righteous son of David is typical of the exilic or post-exilic period.

^{23:1}Woe unto the shepherds that destroy and scatter the sheep of My pasture! saith the Lord.

²Therefore thus saith the Lord, the God of Israel, against the shepherds that feed My people: Ye have scattered My flock, and driven them away, and have not taken care of them; behold, I will visit upon you the evil of your doings, saith the Lord. ³And I will gather the remnant of My flock out of all the countries whither I have driven them, and will bring them back to their folds; and they shall be fruitful and multiply. ⁴And I will set up shepherds over them, who shall feed them; and they shall fear no more, nor be dismayed, neither shall any be lacking, saith the Lord.

⁵Behold, the days come, saith the Lord, that I will raise unto David a righteous shoot, and he shall reign as king and prosper, and shall execute justice and righteousness in the land.

⁶In his days Judah shall be saved, and Israel shall dwell safely; and this is his name whereby he shall be called, the Lord is our righteousness.

⁷Therefore, behold, the days come, saith the Lord, that they shall no more say: 'As the Lord liveth, that brought up the children of Israel out of the land of Egypt'; ⁸but: 'As the Lord liveth, that brought up and that led the seed of the house of Israel out of the north country, and from all the countries whither I had driven them'; and they shall dwell in their own land.

False Prophets (23:9-40)

This is a collection of a number of passages from different times, which are tied together because they are all about false prophets.

Verses 23:16-18 sound like they might be from during the reign of Zedekiah. The false prophets say "'Ye shall have peace'; and unto every one that walketh in the stubbornness of his own heart they say: 'No evil shall come upon you,'" which sounds like it might refer to the prophets who were encouraging the king to break away from Babylon and saying he would not have to worry about Babylon's revenge. However, this dating is uncertain.

By contrast, 23:19-22, with its mention of the "end of days," seems to have been written after Jeremiah's death, during the Babylonian exile, when Messianic expectations were arising.

There is no indication of the dates of the other passages.

23:9Concerning the prophets. My heart within me is broken, all my bones shake; I am like a drunken man, and like a man whom wine hath overcome; because of the Lord, and because of His holy words.

10For the land is full of adulterers; for because of swearing the land mourneth, the pastures of the wilderness are dried up; and their course is evil, and their force is not right.

11For both prophet and priest are ungodly; yea, in My house have I found their wickedness, saith the Lord. 12Wherefore their way shall be unto them as slippery places in the darkness, they shall be thrust, and fall therein; for I will bring evil upon them, even the year of their visitation, saith the Lord.

13And I have seen unseemliness in the prophets of Samaria: they prophesied by Baal, and caused My people Israel to err.

14But in the prophets of Jerusalem I have seen a horrible thing: they commit adultery, and walk in lies, and they strengthen the hands of evil-doers, that none doth return from his wickedness; they are all of them become unto Me as Sodom, and the inhabitants thereof as Gomorrah.

15Therefore thus saith the Lord of hosts concerning the prophets: Behold, I will feed them with wormwood, and make them drink the water of gall; for from the prophets of Jerusalem is ungodliness gone forth into all the land.

16Thus saith the Lord of hosts: Hearken not unto the words of the prophets that prophesy unto you, they lead you unto vanity; they speak a vision of their own heart, and not out of the mouth of the Lord. 17They say continually unto them that despise me: 'The Lord hath said: Ye shall have peace'; and unto every one that walketh in the stubbornness of his own heart they say: 'No evil shall come upon you';

18For who hath stood in the council of the Lord, that he should perceive and hear His word? Who hath attended to His word, and heard it?

[19]Behold, a storm of the Lord is gone forth in fury, yea, a whirling storm; it shall whirl upon the head of the wicked. [20]The anger of the Lord shall not return, until He have executed, and till He have performed the purposes of His heart; in the end of days ye shall consider it perfectly.

[21]I have not sent these prophets, yet they ran; I have not spoken to them, yet they prophesied.

[22]But if they have stood in My council, then let them cause My people to hear My words, and turn them from their evil way, and from the evil of their doings.

[23]Am I a God near at hand, saith the Lord, and not a God afar off? [24]Can any hide himself in secret places that I shall not see him? saith the Lord. Do not I fill heaven and earth? saith the Lord.

[25]I have heard what the prophets have said, that prophesy lies in My name, saying: 'I have dreamed, I have dreamed.'

[26]How long shall this be? Is it in the heart of the prophets that prophesy lies, and the prophets of the deceit of their own heart? [27]That think to cause My people to forget My name by their dreams which they tell every man to his neighbour, as their fathers forgot My name for Baal.

[28]The prophet that hath a dream, let him tell a dream; and he that hath My word, let him speak My word faithfully. What hath the straw to do with the wheat? saith the Lord.

[29]Is not My word like as fire? saith the Lord; and like a hammer that breaketh the rock in pieces?

[30]Therefore, behold, I am against the prophets, saith the Lord, that steal My words every one from his neighbour. [31]Behold, I am against the prophets, saith the Lord, that use their tongues and say: 'He saith.' [32]Behold, I am against them that prophesy lying dreams, saith the Lord, and do tell them, and cause My people to err by their lies, and by their wantonness; yet I sent them not, nor commanded them; neither can they profit this people at all, saith the Lord.

³³And when this people, or the prophet, or a priest, shall ask thee, saying: 'What is the burden of the Lord?' Then shalt thou say unto them: 'What burden! I will cast you off, saith the Lord.' ³⁴And as for the prophet, and the priest, and the people, that shall say: 'The burden of the Lord', I will even punish that man and his house. ³⁵Thus shall ye say every one to his neighbour, and every one to his brother: 'What hath the Lord answered?' and: 'What hath the Lord spoken?' ³⁶And the burden of the Lord shall ye mention no more; for every man's own word shall be his burden; and would ye pervert the words of the living God, of the Lord of hosts our God? ³⁷Thus shalt thou say to the prophet: 'What hath the Lord answered thee?' and: 'What hath the Lord spoken?' ³⁸But if ye say: 'The burden of the Lord'; therefore thus saith the Lord: Because ye say this word: 'The burden of the Lord', and I have sent unto you, saying: 'Ye shall not say: The burden of the Lord'; ³⁹therefore, behold, I will utterly tear you out, and I will cast you off, and the city that I gave unto you and to your fathers, away from My presence; ⁴⁰and I will bring an everlasting reproach upon you, and a perpetual shame, which shall not be forgotten

Destruction of Many Nations (25:11b-38)

Both this passage and most of the Book of Prophecies Against the Nations (46:1-51:64) prophesy the destruction of many nations, including Babylon, and they were probably written after Jeremiah's death, when the Medes or the Persians were moving to conquer Babylon and the entire mid-east. This passage is the conclusion to the Book of 605, and it seems that it was added to that book at about the same time the later parts of the Book of Prophecies against the Nations were being written.

The prophecy of the destruction of Babylon along with the other nations is a bit obscure in this passage, which says: "^{25:17}Then took I the cup of the Lord's hand, and made all the nations to drink ... ^{26b}And the king of Sheshach shall drink after them." Sheshach means Babylon in what is called atbash code, which replaces the first letter of the alphabet with the last letter, the second with the next to the last, and so on. The word Sheshach is used in only two places in the book of Jeremiah: here and in the Book of Prophecies Against the Nations: *"51:41How is Sheshach taken!"*

The beginning of this passage can only be understood as a continuation of the original conclusion of the Book of 605, which reflects conditions in Jeremiah's time by saying:

> *25:7Yet ye have not hearkened unto Me, saith the Lord; that ye might provoke Me with the work of your hands to your own hurt. 8Therefore thus saith the Lord of hosts: Because ye have not heard My words, 9behold, I will send and take all the families of the north, saith the Lord, and I will send unto Nebuchadrezzar the king of Babylon, My servant, and will bring them against this land, and against the inhabitants thereof, and against all these nations round about; and I will utterly destroy them, ... 11aAnd this whole land shall be a desolation, and a waste; ...*

Apparently, the mention here of Nebuchadnezzar devastating the whole land inspired some exilic editor to add this later passage about return from the exile in Babylon and vengeance on the other nations, beginning by continuing the sentence in 25:11a.

25:11b ... and these nations shall serve the king of Babylon seventy years. 12And it shall come to pass, when seventy years are accomplished, that I will punish the king of Babylon, and that nation, saith the Lord, for their iniquity, and the land of the Chaldeans; and I will make it perpetual desolations. 13And I will bring upon that land all My words which I have pronounced against it, even all that is written in this book, which Jeremiah hath prophesied against all the nations. 14For many nations and great kings shall make bondmen of them also; and I will recompense them according to their deeds, and according to the work of their own hands.

15For thus saith the Lord, the God of Israel, unto me: Take this cup of the wine of fury at My hand, and cause all the nations, to whom I send thee, to drink it. 16And they shall drink, and reel to and fro, and be like madmen, because of the sword that I will send among them.—¹⁷Then took I the cup of the Lord's hand, and made all the nations to drink, unto whom the Lord had sent me: ¹⁸Jerusalem, and the cities of Judah, and the kings thereof, and the princes thereof, to make them an appalment, an astonishment, a hissing, and a curse; as it is this day; ¹⁹Pharaoh king of Egypt, and his servants, and his princes, and all his people; ²⁰and all the mingled people; and all the kings of the land of Uz, and all the kings of the land of the Philistines, and Ashkelon, and Gaza, and Ekron, and the remnant of Ashdod; ²¹Edom, and Moab, and the children of Ammon; ²²and all the kings of Tyre, and all the kings of Zidon, and the kings of the isle which is beyond the sea; ²³Dedan, and Tema, and Buz, and all that have the corners of their hair polled; ²⁴and all the kings of Arabia, and all the kings of the mingled people that dwell in the wilderness; ²⁵and all the kings of Zimri, and all the kings of Elam, and all the kings of the Medes; ²⁶and all the kings of the north, far and near, one with another; and all the kingdoms of the world, which are upon the face of the earth.—And the king of Sheshach shall drink after them. ²⁷And thou shalt say unto them: Thus saith the Lord of hosts, the God of Israel: Drink ye, and be drunken, and spew, and fall, and rise no more, because of the sword which I will send among you. ²⁸And it shall be, if they refuse to take the cup at thy hand to drink, then shalt thou say unto them: Thus saith the Lord of hosts: Ye shall surely drink. ²⁹For, lo, I begin to bring evil on the city whereupon My name is called, and should ye be utterly unpunished? Ye shall not be unpunished; for I will call for a sword upon all the inhabitants of the earth, saith the Lord of hosts.

³⁰Therefore prophesy thou against them all these words, and say unto them: The Lord doth roar from on high, And utter His voice from His holy habitation; He doth mightily roar because of His fold; He giveth a shout, as they that tread the grapes, Against all the inhabitants of the earth.

³¹A noise is come even to the end of the earth; For the Lord hath a controversy with the nations, He doth plead with all flesh; As for the wicked, He hath given them to the sword, Saith the Lord.

[32]Thus saith the Lord of hosts: Behold, evil shall go forth From nation to nation, and a great storm shall be raised up from the uttermost parts of the earth.

[33]And the slain of the Lord shall be at that day from one end of the earth even unto the other end of the earth; they shall not be lamented, neither gathered, nor buried; they shall be dung upon the face of the ground.

[34]Wail, ye shepherds, and cry; and wallow yourselves in the dust, ye leaders of the flock; for the days of your slaughter are fully come, and I will break you in pieces, and ye shall fall like a precious vessel.

[35]And the shepherds shall have no way to flee, nor the leaders of the flock to escape.

[36]Hark! the cry of the shepherds, and the wailing of the leaders of the flock! For the Lord despoileth their pasture.

[37]And the peaceable folds are brought to silence because of the fierce anger of the Lord.

[38]He hath forsaken His covert, as the lion; for their land is become a waste because of the fierceness of the oppressing sword, And because of His fierce anger.

The Book of Consolations (Chapters 30-33)

The Book of Consolations is a collection of optimistic prophecies attributed to Jeremiah. Most of it seems to be by a later writer, writing during the exile in Babylon and predicting the return from exile. These predictions do not fit into the historic narrative of Jeremiah's times, and they are not consistent with what Jeremiah was saying at any point in his career.

Scholars have speculated that some parts of it are by Jeremiah, but there are many disagreements about dates and authenticity of passages.

One passage does seem to be an authentic early prophecy by Jeremiah: it begins by describing Rachel weeping for her children and predicts the return of Israel from exile (31:15-22), which is plausibly a prophecy that Jeremiah made during Josiah's reform, when the ten northern tribes of Israel were exiled but Judah was not. This edition includes this passage in the historical narrative.

This edition places the rest of the Book of Consolations in this section. Readers can judge for themselves whether any other passages are actually by Jeremiah.

Return from Exile (30-31:14, 31:23-38)

This part of the Book of Consolation begins by saying that it was written during the captivity of Israel and Judah, and it predicts that both these nations will return from exile. Much of it was clearly written by exiles in Babylon and attributed to Jeremiah.

Some scholars have claimed that Jeremiah wrote parts of this section, but most of the claims are not convincing.

For example, the following passage seems to be a reworking of earlier material that was attributed to Jeremiah though he did not write it:

> 30:23*Behold, a storm of the Lord is gone forth in fury, A sweeping storm; It shall whirl upon the head of the wicked.* 24*The fierce anger of the Lord shall not return, until He have executed, and till He have performed the purposes of His heart; in the end of days ye shall consider it.* 31:1*At that time, saith the Lord, will I be the God of all the families of Israel, and they shall be My people.*

It is very similar to the earlier:

> 23:19*Behold, a storm of the Lord is gone forth in fury, yea, a whirling storm; it shall whirl upon the head of the wicked.* 20*The anger of the Lord shall not return, until He have executed, and till He have performed the purposes of His heart. In the end of days ye shall consider it perfectly.*

Both of these sound like exilic prophecies about a future Messianic age.

Another example is more likely to be a reworking of material that was actually by Jeremiah. Scholars have said that 31:2-6, predicting Israel's return, may have been written by Jeremiah during the years of Josiah's reforms, when he made a number of prophecies about Israel returning. It seems more plausible to read this brief passage as part of the larger post-exilic prophecy that both Israel and Judah would return. But some later editor may have included the earlier material in 31:2-6 as part of this longer prophecy.

30:1The word that came to Jeremiah from the Lord, saying: 2'Thus speaketh the Lord, the God of Israel, saying: Write thee all the words that I have spoken unto thee in a book. 3For, lo, the days come, saith the Lord, that I will turn the captivity of My people Israel and Judah, saith the Lord; and I will cause them to return to the land that I gave to their fathers, and they shall possess it.'

4And these are the words that the Lord spoke concerning Israel and concerning Judah.

⁵For thus saith the Lord: We have heard a voice of trembling, of fear, and not of peace.

⁶Ask ye now, and see whether a man doth travail with child; wherefore do I see every man with his hands on his loins, as a woman in travail, and all faces are turned into paleness?

⁷Alas! For that day is great, so that none is like it; and it is a time of trouble unto Jacob, but out of it shall he be saved. ⁸And it shall come to pass in that day, saith the Lord of hosts, that I will break his yoke from off thy neck, and will burst thy bands; and strangers shall no more make him their bondman; ⁹but they shall serve the Lord their God, and David their king, whom I will raise up unto them.

¹⁰Therefore fear thou not, O Jacob My servant, saith the Lord; neither be dismayed, O Israel; for, lo, I will save thee from afar, and thy seed from the land of their captivity; and Jacob shall again be quiet and at ease, and none shall make him afraid. ¹¹For I am with thee, saith the Lord, to save thee; for I will make a full end of all the nations whither I have scattered thee, but I will not make a full end of thee; for I will correct thee in measure, and will not utterly destroy thee.

¹²For thus saith the Lord: Thy hurt is incurable, and thy wound is grievous. ¹³None deemeth of thy wound that it may be bound up; thou hast no healing medicines. ¹⁴All thy lovers have forgotten thee, they seek thee not; for I have wounded thee with the wound of an enemy, with the chastisement of a cruel one; for the greatness of thine iniquity, because thy sins were increased. ¹⁵Why criest thou for thy hurt, that thy pain is incurable? For the greatness of thine iniquity, because thy sins were increased, I have done these things unto thee.

¹⁶Therefore all they that devour thee shall be devoured, and all thine adversaries, every one of them, shall go into captivity; and they that spoil thee shall be a spoil, and all that prey upon thee will I give for a prey. ¹⁷For I will restore health unto thee, and I will heal thee of thy wounds, saith the Lord; because they have called thee an outcast: 'She is Zion, there is none that careth for her.'

¹⁸Thus saith the Lord: Behold, I will turn the captivity of

Jacob's tents, and have compassion on his dwelling-places; and the city shall be builded upon her own mound, and the palace shall be inhabited upon its wonted place. [19]And out of them shall proceed thanksgiving and the voice of them that make merry; and I will multiply them, and they shall not be diminished, I will also increase them, and they shall not dwindle away.

[20]Their children also shall be as aforetime, and their congregation shall be established before Me, and I will punish all that oppress them. [21]And their prince shall be of themselves, and their ruler shall proceed from the midst of them; and I will cause him to draw near, and he shall approach unto Me; for who is he that hath pledged his heart to approach unto Me? saith the Lord. [22]And ye shall be My people, and I will be your God.

[23]Behold, a storm of the Lord is gone forth in fury, a sweeping storm; it shall whirl upon the head of the wicked. [24]The fierce anger of the Lord shall not return, until He have executed, and till He have performed the purposes of His heart; in the end of days ye shall consider it. [31:1]At that time, saith the Lord, will I be the God of all the families of Israel, and they shall be My people.

[2]Thus saith the Lord: The people that were left of the sword have found grace in the wilderness, even Israel, when I go to cause him to rest.

[3]'From afar the Lord appeared unto me.' 'Yea, I have loved thee with an everlasting love; therefore with affection have I drawn thee. [4]Again will I build thee, and thou shalt be built, O virgin of Israel; again shalt thou be adorned with thy tabrets, and shalt go forth in the dances of them that make merry. [5]Again shalt thou plant vineyards upon the mountains of Samaria; the planters shall plant, and shall have the use thereof.

[6]For there shall be a day, that the watchmen shall call upon the mount Ephraim: Arise ye, and let us go up to Zion, unto the Lord our God.'

[7]For thus saith the Lord: Sing with gladness for Jacob, and shout at the head of the nations; announce ye, praise ye, and say: 'O Lord, save Thy people, the remnant of Israel.' [8]Behold, I will bring them from the north country, and gather them from the uttermost parts of the earth, and with them the blind and the lame,

the woman with child and her that travaileth with child together; a great company shall they return hither. ⁹They shall come with weeping, and with supplications will I lead them; I will cause them to walk by rivers of waters, in a straight way wherein they shall not stumble; for I am become a father to Israel, and Ephraim is My first-born.

¹⁰Hear the word of the Lord, O ye nations, and declare it in the isles afar off, and say: 'He that scattered Israel doth gather him, and keep him, as a shepherd doth his flock.' ¹¹For the Lord hath ransomed Jacob, and He redeemeth him from the hand of him that is stronger than he. ¹²And they shall come and sing in the height of Zion, and shall flow unto the goodness of the Lord, to the corn, and to the wine, and to the oil, and to the young of the flock and of the herd; and their soul shall be as a watered garden, and they shall not pine any more at all.

¹³Then shall the virgin rejoice in the dance, and the young men and the old together; for I will turn their mourning into joy, and will comfort them, and make them rejoice from their sorrow. ¹⁴And I will satiate the soul of the priests with fatness, and My people shall be satisfied with My goodness, saith the Lord.

31:23Thus saith the Lord of hosts, the God of Israel: Yet again shall they use this speech in the land of Judah and in the cities thereof, When I shall turn their captivity: 'The Lord bless thee, O habitation of righteousness, O mountain of holiness.'

²⁴And Judah and all the cities thereof shall dwell therein together: the husbandmen, and they that go forth with flocks. ²⁵For I have satiated the weary soul, and every pining soul have I replenished.

²⁶Upon this I awaked, and beheld; and my sleep was sweet unto me.

²⁷Behold, the days come, saith the Lord, that I will sow the house of Israel and the house of Judah with the seed of man, and with the seed of beast. ²⁸And it shall come to pass, that like as I have watched over them to pluck up and to break down, and to overthrow and to destroy, and to afflict; so will I watch over them

to build and to plant, saith the Lord.

[29]In those days they shall say no more: 'The fathers have eaten sour grapes, and the children's teeth are set on edge.' [30]But every one shall die for his own iniquity; every man that eateth the sour grapes, his teeth shall be set on edge.

[31]Behold, the days come, saith the Lord, that I will make a new covenant with the house of Israel, and with the house of Judah; [32]not according to the covenant that I made with their fathers in the day that I took them by the hand to bring them out of the land of Egypt; forasmuch as they broke My covenant, although I was a lord over them, saith the Lord. [33]But this is the covenant that I will make with the house of Israel after those days, saith the Lord, I will put My law in their inward parts, and in their heart will I write it; and I will be their God, and they shall be My people; [34]and they shall teach no more every man his neighbour, and every man his brother, saying: 'Know the Lord'; for they shall all know Me, from the least of them unto the greatest of them, saith the Lord; for I will forgive their iniquity, and their sin will I remember no more.

[35]Thus saith the Lord, Who giveth the sun for a light by day, and the ordinances of the moon and of the stars for a light by night, Who stirreth up the sea, that the waves thereof roar, the Lord of hosts is His name: [36]If these ordinances depart from before Me, saith the Lord, then the seed of Israel also shall cease from being a nation before Me for ever. [37]Thus saith the Lord: If heaven above can be measured, and the foundations of the earth searched out beneath, then will I also cast off all the seed of Israel for all that they have done, saith the Lord.

[38]Behold, the days come, saith the Lord, that the city shall be built to the Lord from the tower of Hananel unto the gate of the corner. [39]And the measuring line shall yet go out straight forward unto the hill Gareb, and shall turn about unto Goah. [40]And the whole valley of the dead bodies, and of the ashes, and all the fields unto the brook Kidron, unto the corner of the horse gate toward the east, shall be holy unto the Lord; it shall not be plucked up, nor thrown down any more for ever.

First Prophecy from Prison (Chapter 32)

This prophecy, which is part of the Book of Consolations, was supposedly made by Jeremiah when he was imprisoned in the court of the guard late in the reign of Zedekiah, during the siege that occurred before Babylon destroyed Jerusalem completely. He begins by buying a field in Anathoth that was his family's property, and then he prophesies that the Israelites will return to the land after the Babylonians destroy it, so this property will be valuable again. This optimism is inconsistent with what Jeremiah was saying at that time, so it seems that this text was written during the exile and attributed to Jeremiah.

[32:1]The word that came to Jeremiah from the Lord in the tenth year of Zedekiah king of Judah, which was the eighteenth year of Nebuchadrezzar. [2]Now at that time the king of Babylon's army was besieging Jerusalem; and Jeremiah the prophet was shut up in the court of the guard, which was in the king of Judah's house. [3]For Zedekiah king of Judah had shut him up, saying: 'Wherefore dost thou prophesy, and say: Thus saith the Lord: Behold, I will give this city into the hand of the king of Babylon, and he shall take it; [4]and Zedekiah king of Judah shall not escape out of the hand of the Chaldeans, but shall surely be delivered into the hand of the king of Babylon, and shall speak with him mouth to mouth, and his eyes shall behold his eyes; [5]and he shall lead Zedekiah to Babylon, and there shall he be until I remember him, saith the Lord; though ye fight with the Chaldeans, ye shall not prosper?'

[6]And Jeremiah said: 'The word of the Lord came unto me, saying: [7]Behold, Hanamel, the son of Shallum thine uncle, shall come unto thee, saying: Buy thee my field that is in Anathoth; for the right of redemption is thine to buy it.' [8]So Hanamel mine uncle's son came to me in the court of the guard according to the word of the Lord, and said unto me: 'Buy my field, I pray thee, that is in Anathoth, which is in the land of Benjamin; for the right of inheritance is thine, and the redemption is thine; buy it for thyself.' Then I knew that this was the word of the Lord. [9]And I bought the field that was in Anathoth of Hanamel mine uncle's son, and

weighed him the money, even seventeen shekels of silver. [10]And I subscribed the deed, and sealed it, and called witnesses, and weighed him the money in the balances.

[11]So I took the deed of the purchase, both that which was sealed, containing the terms and conditions, and that which was open; [12]and I delivered the deed of the purchase unto Baruch the son of Neriah, the son of Mahseiah, in the presence of Hanamel mine uncle['s son], and in the presence of the witnesses that subscribed the deed of the purchase, before all the Jews that sat in the court of the guard. [13]And I charged Baruch before them, saying: [14]'Thus saith the Lord of hosts, the God of Israel: Take these deeds, this deed of the purchase, both that which is sealed, and this deed which is open, and put them in an earthen vessel; that they may continue many days. [15]For thus saith the Lord of hosts, the God of Israel: Houses and fields and vineyards shall yet again be bought in this land.'

[16]Now after I had delivered the deed of the purchase unto Baruch the son of Neriah, I prayed unto the Lord, saying: [17]'Ah Lord God! behold, Thou hast made the heaven and the earth by Thy great power and by Thy outstretched arm; there is nothing too hard for Thee; [18]who showest mercy unto thousands, and recompensest the iniquity of the fathers into the bosom of their children after them; the great, the mighty God, the Lord of hosts is His name; [19]great in counsel, and mighty in work; whose eyes are open upon all the ways of the sons of men, to give every one according to his ways, and according to the fruit of his doings; [20]who didst set signs and wonders in the land of Egypt, even unto this day, and in Israel and among other men; and madest Thee a name, as at this day; [21]and didst bring forth Thy people Israel out of the land of Egypt with signs, and with wonders, and with a strong hand, and with an outstretched arm, and with great terror; [22]and gavest them this land, which Thou didst swear to their fathers to give them, a land flowing with milk and honey; [23]and they came in, and possessed it; but they hearkened not to Thy voice, neither walked in Thy law; they have done nothing of all that Thou commandedst them to do; therefore Thou hast caused all this evil to befall them; [24]behold the mounds, they are come unto the city to take it; and the city is

given into the hand of the Chaldeans that fight against it, because of the sword, and of the famine, and of the pestilence; and what Thou hast spoken is come to pass; and, behold, Thou seest it. [25]Yet Thou hast said unto me, O Lord God: Buy thee the field for money, and call witnesses; whereas the city is given into the hand of the Chaldeans.'

[26]Then came the word of the Lord unto Jeremiah, saying: [27]'Behold, I am the Lord, the God of all flesh; is there any thing too hard for Me? [28]Therefore thus saith the Lord: Behold, I will give this city into the hand of the Chaldeans, and into the hand of Nebuchadrezzar king of Babylon, and he shall take it; [29]and the Chaldeans, that fight against this city, shall come and set this city on fire, and burn it, with the houses, upon whose roofs they have offered unto Baal, and poured out drink-offerings unto other gods, to provoke Me. [30]For the children of Israel and the children of Judah have only done that which was evil in My sight from their youth; for the children of Israel have only provoked Me with the work of their hands, saith the Lord. [31]For this city hath been to Me a provocation of Mine anger and of My fury from the day that they built it even unto this day, that I should remove it from before My face; [32]because of all the evil of the children of Israel and of the children of Judah, which they have done to provoke Me, they, their kings, their princes, their priests, and their prophets, and the men of Judah, and the inhabitants of Jerusalem. [33]And they have turned unto Me the back, and not the face; and though I taught them, teaching them betimes and often, yet they have not hearkened to receive instruction. [34]But they set their abominations in the house whereupon My name is called, to defile it. [35]And they built the high places of Baal, which are in the valley of the son of Hinnom, to set apart their sons and their daughters unto Molech; which I commanded them not, neither came it into My mind, that they should do this abomination; to cause Judah to sin.

[36]And now therefore thus saith the Lord, the God of Israel, concerning this city, whereof ye say: It is given into the hand of the king of Babylon by the sword, and by the famine, and by the pestilence: [37]Behold, I will gather them out of all the countries, whither I have driven them in Mine anger, and in My fury, and in

great wrath; and I will bring them back unto this place, and I will cause them to dwell safely; [38]and they shall be My people, and I will be their God; [39]and I will give them one heart and one way, that they may fear Me for ever; for the good of them, and of their children after them; [40]and I will make an everlasting covenant with them, that I will not turn away from them, to do them good; and I will put My fear in their hearts, that they shall not depart from Me. [41]Yea, I will rejoice over them to do them good, and I will plant them in this land in truth with My whole heart and with My whole soul.

[42]For thus saith the Lord: Like as I have brought all this great evil upon this people, so will I bring upon them all the good that I have promised them. [43]And fields shall be bought in this land, whereof ye say: It is desolate, without man or beast; it is given into the hand of the Chaldeans. [44]Men shall buy fields for money, and subscribe the deeds, and seal them, and call witnesses, in the land of Benjamin, and in the places about Jerusalem, and in the cities of Judah, and in the cities of the hill-country, and in the cities of the Lowland, and in the cities of the South; for I will cause their captivity to return, saith the Lord.

Second Prophecy from Prison (Chapter 33)

This prophecy also was supposedly made when Jeremiah was in prison late in the reign of Zedekiah. It seems to come at the end of the siege, as it says that buildings have been broken down to form barricades where the Judeans can fight the Babylonians (33:4-5), implying that the Babylonians have already breached the walls of Jerusalem and Judeans are fighting in the streets. Like the first prophecy from prison, it predicts that the Babylonians will devastate Judah but ultimately both Judah and Israel will return from exile and rebuild the land.

Like the first prophecy from prison, it is not consistent with other things that Jeremiah was saying at the time and seems to be a text written during the Babylonian exile and attributed to Jeremiah. It ends with a messianic prophecy that is clearly from the Babylonian exile, saying that a descendent of David will rule justly after over those who returned from exile (33:14-15).

33:1Moreover the word of the Lord came unto Jeremiah the second time, while he was yet shut up in the court of the guard, saying:

2Thus saith the Lord the Maker thereof, The Lord that formed it to establish it, The Lord is His name: 3Call unto Me, and I will answer thee, and will tell thee great things, and hidden, which thou knowest not.

4For thus saith the Lord, the God of Israel, concerning the houses of this city, and concerning the houses of the kings of Judah, which are broken down for mounds, and for ramparts; 5whereon they come to fight with the Chaldeans, even to fill them with the dead bodies of men, whom I have slain in Mine anger and in My fury, and for all whose wickedness I have hid My face from this city:

6Behold, I will bring it healing and cure, and I will cure them; and I will reveal unto them the abundance of peace and truth. 7And I will cause the captivity of Judah and the captivity of Israel to return, and will build them, as at the first. 8And I will cleanse them from all their iniquity, whereby they have sinned against Me; and I will pardon all their iniquities, whereby they have sinned against Me, and whereby they have transgressed against Me. 9And this city shall be to Me for a name of joy, for a praise and for a glory, before all the nations of the earth, which shall hear all the good that I do unto them, and shall fear and tremble for all the good and for all the peace that I procure unto it.

10Thus saith the Lord: Yet again there shall be heard in this place, whereof ye say: It is waste, without man and without beast, even in the cities of Judah, and in the streets of Jerusalem, that are desolate, without man and without inhabitant and without beast, 11the voice of joy and the voice of gladness, the voice of the bridegroom and the voice of the bride, the voice of them that say: 'Give thanks to the Lord of hosts, for the Lord is good, for His mercy endureth for ever', even of them that bring offerings of thanksgiving into the house of the Lord. For I will cause the captivity of the land to return as at the first, saith the Lord.

[12]Thus saith the Lord of hosts: Yet again shall there be in this place, which is waste, without man and without beast, and in all the cities thereof, a habitation of shepherds causing their flocks to lie down. [13]In the cities of the hill-country, in the cities of the Lowland, and in the cities of the South, and in the land of Benjamin, and in the places about Jerusalem, and in the cities of Judah, shall the flocks again pass under the hands of him that counteth them, saith the Lord.

[14]Behold, the days come, saith the Lord, that I will perform that good word which I have spoken concerning the house of Israel and concerning the house of Judah.

[15]In those days, and at that time, Will I cause a shoot of righteousness to grow up unto David; And he shall execute justice and righteousness in the land.

[16]In those days shall Judah be saved, and Jerusalem shall dwell safely; and this is the name whereby she shall be called, The Lord is our righteousness.

[17]For thus saith the Lord: There shall not be cut off unto David a man to sit upon the throne of the house of Israel; [18]neither shall there be cut off unto the priests the Levites a man before Me to offer burnt-offerings, and to burn meal-offerings, and to do sacrifice continually.

[19]And the word of the Lord came unto Jeremiah, saying: [20]Thus saith the Lord: If ye can break My covenant with the day, and My covenant with the night, so that there should not be day and night in their season; [21]then may also My covenant be broken with David My servant, that he should not have a son to reign upon his throne; and with the Levites the priests, My ministers. [22]As the host of heaven cannot be numbered, neither the sand of the sea measured; so will I multiply the seed of David My servant, and the Levites that minister unto Me.

[23]And the word of the Lord came to Jeremiah, saying: [24]'Considerest thou not what this people have spoken, saying: The two families which the Lord did choose, He hath cast them off? and they contemn My people, that they should be no more a nation before them. [25]Thus saith the Lord: If My covenant be not with day and night, if I have not appointed the ordinances of heaven and

earth; [26]then will I also cast away the seed of Jacob, and of David My servant, so that I will not take of his seed to be rulers over the seed of Abraham, Isaac, and Jacob; for I will cause their captivity to return, and will have compassion on them.'

Prophecies Against the Nations
(Chapters 46-51)

This book of prophecies against the nations is set off very clearly from the rest of the book of Jeremiah. It begins with "⁴⁶:¹The word of the Lord which came to Jeremiah the prophet concerning the nations," and it ends with "⁵¹:⁶⁴ᵇThus far are the words of Jeremiah." The Hebrew word translated as "nations" is commonly used to mean all the nations except Israel, and it can also be translated as "gentiles."

The first two prophecies of this book, about the defeat and destruction of Egypt, seem authentic, since Jeremiah's major concern during much of his career was to convince Judah to submit to Babylon rather than allying with Egypt against Babylon. These are included in the historical narrative.

The final prophecy, about the destruction of Babylon (chapters 50 and 51), and the anecdote that follows (51:59-64a) about Jeremiah sending this prophecy to be read in Babylon during the fourth year of the reign of Zedekiah, are clearly inauthentic. Jeremiah spent most of his career preaching that Judah should submit to Babylon to avoid destruction. This passage describes an event that supposedly happened when Jeremiah was wearing a yoke to symbolize his support for submission. It is not at all plausible that Jeremiah would prophesy the destruction of Babylon at this time, undermining his advice to submit to them, and have the prophecy read in Babylon, endangering the peaceful relationship between the two countries.

Apart from the first two prophecies about Egypt, it seems very unlikely that any of these prophecies against the nations were written by Jeremiah: they were written after Jeremiah's death, perhaps incorporating earlier texts, and they were attributed to Jeremiah. Scholars have connected other parts of this lengthy prophecy with historic events and speculated that Jeremiah made these prophecies at the time of these events. But the prophecies do not fit into the historical narrative of Jeremiah's life and do not reflect Jeremiah's actual concerns at the time of these events.

These prophecies are in a different order and a different location in the Septuagint's version of the Book of Jeremiah, indicating that they were combined and added to the book of Jeremiah late. It seems plausible that a group of Jeremiah's followers preserved the two prophecies of the destruction of Egypt, and during the Babylonian exile, wrote follow-up prophecies about the destruction of other nations—and that all these prophecies were ultimately combined to form this book.

Apart from the two prophecies about Egypt, which are included in the historical narrative, this edition keeps all the prophecies against the nations in this separate section, with notes on how scholars have connected the prophecies with events that happened during Jeremiah's life, so readers can judge for themselves whether they might be authentic.

Superscript (46:1)

The superscript sets off the beginning of the book.

⁴⁶:¹The word of the Lord which came to Jeremiah the prophet concerning the nations.

Against Egypt (46:25-28)

This prophecy seems much less typical of Jeremiah than the first two prophecies against Egypt, and it seems much more like the bulk of the prophecies against the nations, where God is punishing the nations. Conceivably, the prediction of the return of Israel from captivity (46:27) might have been written by Jeremiah during the period of Josiah's reform, and incorporated in this later prophecy against Egypt.

"Amon of No" refers to the god Amon, who was worshipped in the Egyptian city of No, which the Greeks called Thebes.

46:25The Lord of hosts, the God of Israel, saith: Behold, I will punish Amon of No, and Pharaoh, and Egypt, with her gods, and her kings; even Pharaoh, and them that trust in him; 26and I will deliver them into the hand of those that seek their lives, and into the hand of Nebuchadrezzar king of Babylon, and into the hand of his servants; and afterwards it shall be inhabited, as in the days of old, saith the Lord.

27But fear not thou, O Jacob My servant, neither be dismayed, O Israel; for, lo, I will save thee from afar, and thy seed from the land of their captivity; and Jacob shall again be quiet and at ease, and none shall make him afraid.

28Fear not thou, O Jacob My servant, saith the Lord, for I am with thee; for I will make a full end of all the nations whither I have driven thee, but I will not make a full end of thee; and I will correct thee in measure, but will not utterly destroy thee.

Against the Philistines (47:1-7)

The Philistines lived in Gaza, west of Judah. This prophecy is not included in the Septuagint, so it is probably a late addition. This is a typical prophecy against the nations, predicting God's vengeance on one of the surrounding peoples.

47:1The word of the Lord that came to Jeremiah the prophet concerning the Philistines, before that Pharaoh smote Gaza.

2Thus saith the Lord: Behold, waters rise up out of the north, and shall become an overflowing stream, and they shall overflow the land and all that is therein, the city and them that dwell therein; and the men shall cry, and all the inhabitants of the land shall wail.

3At the noise of the stamping of the hoofs of his strong ones, at the rushing of his chariots, at the rumbling of his wheels, the fathers look not back to their children for feebleness of hands; [4]because of the day that cometh to spoil all the Philistines, to cut off from Tyre and Zidon every helper that remaineth; for the Lord will spoil the Philistines, the remnant of the isle of Caphtor.

[5]Baldness is come upon Gaza, Ashkelon is brought to nought, the remnant of their valley; how long wilt thou cut thyself? [6]O thou sword of the Lord, how long will it be ere thou be quiet? Put up thyself into thy scabbard, rest, and be still. [7]How canst thou be quiet? For the Lord hath given it a charge; against Ashkelon, and against the sea-shore, there hath He appointed it.

Against Moab (48:1-47)

Moab and Ammon are east of Judah. Scholars have speculated that this prophecy about Moab and the prophecy about Ammon that follows it may refer to the time when Zedekiah discussed rebellion against Babylon with Moab and Ammon in 594 (27:3) or to the time when Nebuchadnezzar marched against Moab and Ammon in 582, or that this prophecy may refer to the time shortly afterwards when Moab was destroyed by Arab invaders. But it is best understood another typical prophecy against the nations, predicting the destruction of all the surrounding peoples.

[48:1]Of Moab. Thus saith the Lord of hosts, the God of Israel: Woe unto Nebo! for it is spoiled; Kiriathaim is put to shame, it is taken; Misgab is put to shame and dismayed.

[2]The praise of Moab is no more; in Heshbon they have devised evil against her: 'Come, and let us cut her off from being a nation.' Thou also, O Madmen, shalt be brought to silence; the sword shall pursue thee.

[3]Hark! a cry from Horonaim, spoiling and great destruction! [4]Moab is destroyed; her little ones have caused a cry to be heard. [5]For by the ascent of Luhith with continual weeping shall they go up; for in the going down of Horonaim they have heard the distressing cry of destruction.

[6]Flee, save your lives, and be like a tamarisk in the wilderness.

⁷For, because thou hast trusted in thy works and in thy treasures, thou also shalt be taken; and Chemosh shall go forth into captivity, his priests and his princes together. ⁸And the spoiler shall come upon every city, and no city shall escape; the valley also shall perish, and the plain shall be destroyed; as the Lord hath spoken.

⁹Give wings unto Moab, for she must fly and get away; and her cities shall become a desolation, without any to dwell therein.

¹⁰Cursed be he that doeth the work of the Lord with a slack hand, and cursed be he that keepeth back his sword from blood.

¹¹Moab hath been at ease from his youth, and he hath settled on his lees, and hath not been emptied from vessel to vessel, neither hath he gone into captivity; therefore his taste remaineth in him, And his scent is not changed.

¹²Therefore, behold, the days come, saith the Lord, that I will send unto him them that tilt up, and they shall tilt him up; and they shall empty his vessels, and break their bottles in pieces. ¹³And Moab shall be ashamed of Chemosh, as the house of Israel was ashamed of Beth-el their confidence.

¹⁴How say ye: 'We are mighty men, and valiant men for the war'? ¹⁵Moab is spoiled, and they are gone up into her cities, and his chosen young men are gone down to the slaughter, saith the King, Whose name is the Lord of hosts.

¹⁶The calamity of Moab is near to come, and his affliction hasteth fast. ¹⁷Bemoan him, all ye that are round about him, and all ye that know his name; say: 'How is the strong staff broken, the beautiful rod!'

¹⁸O thou daughter that dwellest in Dibon, come down from thy glory, and sit in thirst; for the spoiler of Moab is come up against thee, he hath destroyed thy strongholds. ¹⁹O inhabitant of Aroer, stand by the way, and watch; ask him that fleeth, and her that escapeth; say: 'What hath been done?'

²⁰Moab is put to shame, for it is dismayed; wail and cry; tell ye it in Arnon, that Moab is spoiled. ²¹And judgment is come upon the country of the Plain; upon Holon, and upon Jahzah, and upon Mephaath; ²²and upon Dibon, and upon Nebo, and upon Beth-diblathaim; ²³and upon Kiriathaim, and upon Beth-gamul, and

upon Beth-meon; ²⁴and upon Kerioth, and upon Bozrah, and upon all the cities of the land of Moab, far or near.

²⁵The horn of Moab is cut off, and his arm is broken, Saith the Lord.

²⁶Make ye him drunken, for he magnified himself against the Lord; and Moab shall wallow in his vomit, and he also shall be in derision. ²⁷For was not Israel a derision unto thee? Was he found among thieves? For as often as thou speakest of him, thou waggest the head.

²⁸O ye that dwell in Moab, leave the cities, and dwell in the rock; and be like the dove that maketh her nest in the sides of the pit's mouth.

²⁹We have heard of the pride of Moab; he is very proud; his loftiness, and his pride, and his haughtiness, and the assumption of his heart. ³⁰I know his arrogancy, saith the Lord, that it is ill-founded; his boastings have wrought nothing well-founded. ³¹Therefore will I wail for Moab; yea, I will cry out for all Moab; for the men of Kir-heres shall my heart moan. ³²With more than the weeping of Jazer will I weep for thee, O vine of Sibmah; thy branches passed over the sea, they reached even to the sea of Jazer; upon thy summer fruits and upon thy vintage the spoiler is fallen. ³³And gladness and joy is taken away from the fruitful field, and from the land of Moab; and I have caused wine to cease from the winepresses; none shall tread with shouting; the shouting shall be no shouting.

³⁴From the cry of Heshbon even unto Elealeh, even unto Jahaz have they uttered their voice, from Zoar even unto Horonaim, a heifer of three years old; for the Waters of Nimrim also shall be desolate. ³⁵Moreover I will cause to cease in Moab, saith the Lord, him that offereth in the high place, and him that offereth to his gods.

³⁶Therefore my heart moaneth for Moab like pipes, and my heart moaneth like pipes for the men of Kir-heres; therefore the abundance that he hath gotten is perished. ³⁷For every head is bald, and every beard clipped; upon all the hands are cuttings, and upon the loins sackcloth. ³⁸On all the housetops of Moab and in the

broad places thereof there is lamentation every where; for I have broken Moab like a vessel wherein is no pleasure, saith the Lord.

[39]'How is it broken down!' wail ye! 'How hath Moab turned the back with shame!' So shall Moab become a derision and a dismay to all that are round about him.

[40]For thus saith the Lord: Behold, he shall swoop as a vulture, and shall spread out his wings against Moab. [41]The cities are taken, and the strongholds are seized, and the heart of the mighty men of Moab at that day shall be as the heart of a woman in her pangs. [42]And Moab shall be destroyed from being a people, because he hath magnified himself against the Lord.

[43]Terror, and the pit, and the trap, are upon thee, O inhabitant of Moab, saith the Lord. [44]He that fleeth from the terror shall fall into the pit; and he that getteth up out of the pit shall be taken in the trap; for I will bring upon her, even upon Moab, the year of their visitation, saith the Lord.

[45]In the shadow of Heshbon the fugitives stand without strength; for a fire is gone forth out of Heshbon, and a flame from the midst of Sihon, and it devoureth the corner of Moab, and the crown of the head of the tumultuous ones.

[46]Woe unto thee, O Moab! The people of Chemosh is undone; for thy sons are taken away captive, and thy daughters into captivity.

[47]Yet will I turn the captivity of Moab In the end of days, saith the Lord. Thus far is the judgment of Moab.

Against Ammon (49:1-6)

Scholars have speculated that this prophecy might refer to several different historic situations, like the prophecy against Moab. But it is best understood as another typical prophecy against the nations, predicting the destruction of the peoples surrounding Israel.

Moab and Ammon were east of the Jordan River, with Moab to the north of Ammon. One interesting part of this passage is the prophecy that, after Ammon is destroyed, "[48:2]... Then shall Israel dispossess them that did dispossess him." Moab took possession

*of the territory of Gad, one of the Israelite tribes that settled east
of the Jordan, and this verse predicts that this Israelite tribe,
currently exiled in Assyria, will return and take its land back.*

[49:1]Of the children of Ammon. Thus saith the Lord: Hath Israel no
sons? Hath he no heir? Why then doth Malcam take possession of
Gad, and his people dwell in the cities thereof?

[2]Therefore, behold, the days come, saith the Lord, that I will
cause an alarm of war to be heard against Rabbah of the children of
Ammon; and it shall become a desolate mound, and her daughters
shall be burned with fire; then shall Israel dispossess them that
did dispossess him, saith the Lord. [3]Wail, O Heshbon, for Ai is
undone; cry, ye daughters of Rabbah, gird you with sackcloth;
lament, and run to and fro among the folds; for Malcam shall go
into captivity, his priests and his princes together.

[4]Wherefore gloriest thou in the valleys, thy flowing valley, O
backsliding daughter? That didst trust in thy treasures: 'Who shall
come unto me?' [5]Behold, I will bring a terror upon thee, saith the
Lord God of hosts, from all that are round about thee; and ye shall
be driven out every man right forth, and there shall be none to
gather up him that wandereth.

[6]But afterward I will bring back the captivity of the children of
Ammon, saith the Lord.

Against Edom (49:7-22)

*Edom is to the south of Judah. Scholars have suggested that this
was written because Edom (like Moab and Ammon) were plotting
against Babylon early in Zedekiah's reign (27:3), but it is best
understood as just another typical prophecy predicting destruction
of all the surrounding nations. The prophecy refers to Edom using
the name of Jacob's brother Esau, who was supposed to be the
ancestor of Edom.*

[49:7]Of Edom. Thus saith the Lord of hosts: Is wisdom no more in
Teman? Is counsel perished from the prudent? Is their wisdom

vanished? [8]Flee ye, turn back, dwell deep, O inhabitants of Dedan; for I do bring the calamity of Esau upon him, the time that I shall punish him.

[9]If grape-gatherers came to thee, would they not leave some gleaning grapes? If thieves by night, would they not destroy till they had enough? [10]But I have made Esau bare, I have uncovered his secret places, and he shall not be able to hide himself; his seed is spoiled, and his brethren, and his neighbours, and he is not.

[11]Leave thy fatherless children, I will rear them, and let thy widows trust in Me. [12]For thus saith the Lord: Behold, they to whom it pertained not to drink of the cup shall assuredly drink; and art thou he that shall altogether go unpunished? Thou shalt not go unpunished, but thou shalt surely drink. [13]For I have sworn by Myself, saith the Lord, that Bozrah shall become an astonishment, a reproach, a waste, and a curse; and all the cities thereof shall be perpetual wastes.

[14]I have heard a message from the Lord, and an ambassador is sent among the nations: 'Gather yourselves together, and come against her, and rise up to the battle.' [15]For, behold, I make thee small among the nations, and despised among men.

[16]Thy terribleness hath deceived thee, even the pride of thy heart, O thou that dwellest in the clefts of the rock, that holdest the height of the hill; though thou shouldest make thy nest as high as the eagle, I will bring thee down from thence, saith the Lord. [17]And Edom shall become an astonishment; every one that passeth by it shall be astonished and shall hiss at all the plagues thereof. [18]As in the overthrow of Sodom and Gomorrah and the neighbour cities thereof, saith the Lord, no man shall abide there, neither shall any son of man dwell therein.

[19]Behold, he shall come up like a lion from the thickets of the Jordan against the strong habitation; for I will suddenly make him run away from it, and whoso is chosen, him will I appoint over it; for who is like Me? And who will appoint Me a time? And who is that shepherd that will stand before Me?

[20]Therefore hear ye the counsel of the Lord, that He hath taken against Edom; and His purposes, that He hath purposed against the

inhabitants of Teman: surely the least of the flock shall drag them away, surely their habitation shall be appalled at them. [21]The earth quaketh at the noise of their fall; there is a cry, the noise whereof is heard in the Red Sea. [22]Behold, he shall come up and swoop down as the vulture, and spread out his wings against Bozrah; and the heart of the mighty men of Edom at that day shall be as the heart of a woman in her pangs.

Against Damascus (49:23-27)

Scholars say we do not know enough history to suggest a date for this prophecy, though we do know that the Syrians were allied with Babylon in its campaign against Judah during the time of Jehoiakim and the prophecy might refer to this time. But it is best understood as another typical prophecy of the destruction of all the surrounding nations, attributed to Jeremiah though it was written after his time.

[49:23]Of Damascus. Hamath is ashamed, and Arpad; for they have heard evil tidings, they are melted away; there is trouble in the sea; It cannot be quiet. [24]Damascus is waxed feeble, she turneth herself to flee, and trembling hath seized on her; anguish and pangs have taken hold of her, as of a woman in travail.

[25]'How is the city of praise left unrepaired, the city of my joy?'

[26]Therefore her young men shall fall in her broad places, and all the men of war shall be brought to silence in that day, saith the Lord of hosts. [27]And I will kindle a fire in the wall of Damascus, and it shall devour the palaces of Ben-hadad.

Against Kedar and Hazor (49:28-33)

Kedar (now usually spelled Qedar) was a powerful kingdom of Arab tribes that lived to the southeast of Judah, and Hazor was a once-powerful Canaanite city to the northeast. The Babylonian chronicle tells us that Nebuchadnezzar conquered Kedar and other Arab tribes in 599-598, giving us some idea of the time frame 49:28 refers to. Presumably, Kedar and Hazor are connected here because the Babylonians conquered them both at about the same time.

This passage does not seem to have any connection with Jeremiah's concerns or history, though it supports his belief in inevitable Babylonian victory. It is probably best understood as just another prophecy against the nations, which uses the Babylonian victory over Kedar and Hazor to make the usual point that all the nations surrounding Judah will be destroyed.

[49:28]Of Kedar, and of the kingdoms of Hazor, which Nebuchadrezzar king of Babylon smote.

Thus saith the Lord: Arise ye, go up against Kedar, And spoil the children of the east. [29]Their tents and their flocks shall they take, they shall carry away for themselves their curtains, and all their vessels, and their camels; and they shall proclaim against them a terror on every side.

[30]Flee ye, flit far off, dwell deep, O ye inhabitants of Hazor, saith the Lord; For Nebuchadrezzar king of Babylon hath taken counsel against you, And hath conceived a purpose against you. [31]Arise, get you up against a nation that is at ease, that dwelleth without care, saith the Lord; that have neither gates nor bars, that dwell alone. [32]And their camels shall be a booty, and the multitude of their cattle a spoil; and I will scatter unto all winds them that have the corners polled; and I will bring their calamity from every side of them, saith the Lord. [33]And Hazor shall be a dwelling-place of jackals, a desolation for ever; no man shall abide there, neither shall any son of man dwell therein.

Against Elam (49:34-39)

Elam was a nation located east of where the Tigris flows into the Persian gulf—east of Mesopotamia, where Babylon was located, and thus further from Judah than Babylon. The Israelites believed that the Elamites were descendents of Elam son of Shem son of

Noah (Genesis 10:22), which means they considered Elam to be Semitic, but its language was not Semitic.

This prophecy begins by dating itself "in the beginning of the reign of Zedekiah," but it does not seem to have anything to do with Jeremiah's interests at that time. It is best understood as another typical exilic prophecy against the nations, predicting the destruction of all the surrounding peoples, with the dating included to support the attribution to Jeremiah.

49:34The word of the Lord that came to Jeremiah the prophet concerning Elam in the beginning of the reign of Zedekiah king of Judah, saying: 35Thus saith the Lord of hosts: Behold, I will break the bow of Elam the chief of their might. 36and I will bring against Elam the four winds from the four quarters of heaven, and will scatter them toward all those winds; and there shall be no nation whither the dispersed of Elam shall not come.

37And I will cause Elam to be dismayed before their enemies, and before them that seek their life; and I will bring evil upon them, even My fierce anger, saith the Lord; and I will send the sword after them, till I have consumed them; 38and I will set My throne in Elam, and will destroy from thence king and princes, saith the Lord.

39But it shall come to pass in the end of days, that I will bring back the captivity of Elam, saith the Lord.

Babylon Will Fall and Exiles Return (50:1-51:58)

The book culminates with the longest and fiercest of the prophecies against the nations, the prophecy of the destruction of Babylon. Jeremiah spent much of his career predicting the victory of Babylon in order to convince Judah to accept its yoke, so it is not plausible that he would have predicted the destruction of Babylon. This passage claims that God is taking vengeance on Babylon for conquering Judah, just the opposite of Jeremiah's claim that God willed Babylon to conquer Judah (27:6). Clearly, this is a later text that was ascribed to Jeremiah, like most of the prophecies against the nations.

It seems to have been written when the Medes (51:11, 28) were threatening to conquer Babylon. In fact, it was the Persian king Cyrus the Great, rather than the Medes, who conquered Babylon in 539 and allowed the Judean exiles to return. Cyrus was initially a Median vassal, but he rebelled in 553 and won a decisive victory over the Medes in 550. This passage was presumably written before Cyrus' victory, when the Medes still seemed more powerful.

In "⁵¹:⁴¹How is Sheshach taken!" the word Sheshach means Babylon, using atbash code where the last letter of the alphabet replaces the first, the next to the last replaces the second, and so on. Sheshach is used in two passages that are both later additions the Book of Jeremiah, here and in 25:26.

⁵⁰:¹The word that the Lord spoke concerning Babylon, concerning the land of the Chaldeans, by Jeremiah the prophet.

²Declare ye among the nations and announce, and set up a standard; announce, and conceal not; say: 'Babylon is taken, Bel is put to shame, Merodach is dismayed; her images are put to shame, her idols are dismayed.' ³For out of the north there cometh up a nation against her, which shall make her land desolate, and none shall dwell therein; they are fled, they are gone, both man and beast.

⁴In those days, and in that time, saith the Lord, the children of Israel shall come, they and the children of Judah together; they shall go on their way weeping, and shall seek the Lord their God. ⁵They shall inquire concerning Zion with their faces hitherward: 'Come ye, and join yourselves to the Lord in an everlasting covenant that shall not be forgotten.'

⁶My people hath been lost sheep; their shepherds have caused them to go astray, they have turned them away on the mountains; they have gone from mountain to hill, they have forgotten their resting-place. ⁷All that found them have devoured them; and their adversaries said: 'We are not guilty'; because they have sinned against the Lord, the habitation of justice, even the Lord, the hope of their fathers.

⁸Flee out of the midst of Babylon, and go forth out of the land of the Chaldeans, and be as the he-goats before the flocks. ⁹For, lo,

I will stir up and cause to come up against Babylon an assembly of great nations from the north country; and they shall set themselves in array against her, from thence she shall be taken; their arrows shall be as of a mighty man that maketh childless; none shall return in vain. ¹⁰And Chaldea shall be a spoil; all that spoil her shall be satisfied, saith the Lord.

¹¹Because ye are glad, because ye rejoice, O ye that plunder My heritage, because ye gambol as a heifer at grass, And neigh as strong horses; ¹²your mother shall be sore ashamed, she that bore you shall be confounded; behold, the hindermost of the nations shall be a wilderness, a dry land, and a desert. ¹³Because of the wrath of the Lord it shall not be inhabited, but it shall be wholly desolate; every one that goeth by Babylon shall be appalled and hiss at all her plagues.

¹⁴Set yourselves in array against Babylon round about, all ye that bend the bow, shoot at her, spare no arrows; for she hath sinned against the Lord. ¹⁵Shout against her round about, she hath submitted herself; her buttresses are fallen, her walls are thrown down; for it is the vengeance of the Lord, take vengeance upon her; as she hath done, do unto her.

¹⁶Cut off the sower from Babylon, and him that handleth the sickle in the time of harvest; for fear of the oppressing sword they shall turn every one to his people, and they shall flee every one to his own land.

¹⁷Israel is a scattered sheep, the lions have driven him away; first the king of Assyria hath devoured him, and last this Nebuchadrezzar king of Babylon hath broken his bones. ¹⁸Therefore thus saith the Lord of hosts, the God of Israel: behold, I will punish the king of Babylon and his land, as I have punished the king of Assyria. ¹⁹And I will bring Israel back to his pasture, and he shall feed on Carmel and Bashan, and his soul shall be satisfied upon the hills of Ephraim and in Gilead. ²⁰In those days, and in that time, saith the Lord, the iniquity of Israel shall be sought for, and there shall be none, and the sins of Judah, and they shall not be found; for I will pardon them whom I leave as a remnant.

²¹Go up against the land of Merathaim, even against it, and against the inhabitants of Pekod; waste and utterly destroy after

them, saith the Lord, and do according to all that I have commanded thee. [22]Hark! Battle is in the land, and great destruction. [23]How is the hammer of the whole earth cut asunder and broken! How is Babylon become a desolation among the nations!

[24]I have laid a snare for thee, and thou art also taken, O Babylon, and thou wast not aware; thou art found, and also caught, because thou hast striven against the Lord. [25]The Lord hath opened His armoury, and hath brought forth the weapons of His indignation; for it is a work that the Lord God of hosts hath to do in the land of the Chaldeans.

[26]Come against her from every quarter, open her granaries, cast her up as heaps, and destroy her utterly; let nothing of her be left. [27]Slay all her bullocks, let them go down to the slaughter; woe unto them! for their day is come, the time of their visitation.

[28]Hark! They flee and escape out of the land of Babylon, to declare in Zion the vengeance of the Lord our God, the vengeance of His temple. [29]Call together the archers against Babylon, all them that bend the bow; encamp against her round about, let none thereof escape; recompense her according to her work, according to all that she hath done, do unto her: for she hath been arrogant against the Lord, against the Holy One of Israel. [30]Therefore shall her young men fall in her broad places, and all her men of war shall be brought to silence in that day, saith the Lord.

[31]Behold, I am against thee, O thou most arrogant, saith the Lord God of hosts; for thy day is come, the time that I will punish thee. [32]And the most arrogant shall stumble and fall, and none shall raise him up; and I will kindle a fire in his cities, and it shall devour all that are round about him.

[33]Thus saith the Lord of hosts: The children of Israel and the children of Judah are oppressed together; and all that took them captives hold them fast; they refuse to let them go. [34]Their Redeemer is strong, the Lord of hosts is His name; He will thoroughly plead their cause, that He may give rest to the earth, and disquiet the inhabitants of Babylon.

[35]A sword is upon the Chaldeans, saith the Lord, and upon the inhabitants of Babylon, and upon her princes, and upon her wise

men. ³⁶A sword is upon the boasters, and they shall become fools; a sword is upon her mighty men, and they shall be dismayed. ³⁷A sword is upon their horses, and upon their chariots, and upon all the mingled people that are in the midst of her, and they shall become as women; a sword is upon her treasures, and they shall be robbed.

³⁸A drought is upon her waters, and they shall be dried up; for it is a land of graven images, and they are mad upon things of horror. ³⁹Therefore the wild-cats with the jackals shall dwell there, and the ostriches shall dwell therein; and it shall be no more inhabited for ever, neither shall it be dwelt in from generation to generation. ⁴⁰As when God overthrew Sodom and Gomorrah and the neighbour cities thereof, saith the Lord; so shall no man abide there, neither shall any son of man dwell therein.

⁴¹Behold, a people cometh from the north, and a great nation, and many kings shall be roused from the uttermost parts of the earth. ⁴²They lay hold on bow and spear, they are cruel, and have no compassion; their voice is like the roaring sea, and they ride upon horses; set in array, as a man for war, against thee, O daughter of Babylon. ⁴³The king of Babylon hath heard the fame of them, and his hands wax feeble; anguish hath taken hold of him, and pain, as of a woman in travail.

⁴⁴Behold, he shall come up like a lion from the thickets of the Jordan against the strong habitation; for I will suddenly make them run away from it, and whoso is chosen, him will I appoint over it; for who is like Me? and who will appoint Me a time? And who is that shepherd that will stand before Me?

⁴⁵Therefore hear ye the counsel of the Lord, that He hath taken against Babylon, and His purposes, that He hath purposed against the land of the Chaldeans: surely the least of the flock shall drag them away, surely their habitation shall be appalled at them. ⁴⁶At the noise of the taking of Babylon the earth quaketh, and the cry is heard among the nations.

⁵¹:¹Thus saith the Lord: Behold, I will raise up against Babylon, and against them that dwell in Lebkamai, a destroying wind. ²And I will send unto Babylon strangers, that shall fan her, and they

shall empty her land; for in the day of trouble they shall be against her round about. ³Let the archer bend his bow against her, and let him lift himself up against her in his coat of mail; and spare ye not her young men, destroy ye utterly all her host. ⁴And they shall fall down slain in the land of the Chaldeans, and thrust through in her streets.

⁵For Israel is not widowed, nor Judah, of his God, of the Lord of hosts; for their land is full of guilt against the Holy One of Israel. ⁶Flee out of the midst of Babylon, and save every man his life, be not cut off in her iniquity; for it is the time of the Lord's vengeance; He will render unto her a recompense.

⁷Babylon hath been a golden cup in Lord's hand, that made all the earth drunken; the nations have drunk of her wine, therefore the nations are mad. ⁸Babylon is suddenly fallen and destroyed, wail for her; take balm for her pain, if so be she may be healed.

⁹We would have healed Babylon, but she is not healed; forsake her, and let us go every one into his own country; for her judgment reacheth unto heaven, and is lifted up even to the skies. ¹⁰The Lord hath brought forth our victory; come, and let us declare in Zion the work of the Lord our God.

¹¹Make bright the arrows, fill the quivers, the Lord hath roused the spirit of the kings of the Medes; because His device is against Babylon, to destroy it; for it is the vengeance of the Lord, the vengeance of His temple. ¹²Set up a standard against the walls of Babylon, make the watch strong, set the watchmen, prepare the ambushes; for the Lord hath both devised and done that which He spoke concerning the inhabitants of Babylon.

¹³O thou that dwellest upon many waters, abundant in treasures, thine end is come, the measure of thy covetousness.

¹⁴The Lord of hosts hath sworn by Himself: Surely I will fill thee with men, as with the canker-worm, and they shall lift up a shout against thee. ¹⁵He that hath made the earth by His power, that hath established the world by His wisdom, and hath stretched out the heavens by His discernment; ¹⁶at the sound of His giving a multitude of waters in the heavens, He causeth the vapours to ascend from the ends of the earth; He maketh

lightnings at the time of the rain, and bringeth forth the wind out of His treasuries;

¹⁷Every man is proved to be brutish, for the knowledge—every goldsmith is put to shame by the graven image—that his molten image is falsehood, and there is no breath in them. ¹⁸They are vanity, a work of delusion; in the time of their visitation they shall perish, ¹⁹the portion of Jacob is not like these; for He is the former of all things, and [Israel] is the tribe of His inheritance; the Lord of hosts is His name.

²⁰Thou art My maul and weapons of war, and with thee will I shatter the nations, and with thee will I destroy kingdoms; ²¹and with thee will I shatter the horse and his rider, and with thee will I shatter the chariot and him that rideth therein; ²²and with thee will I shatter man and woman, and with thee will I shatter the old man and the youth, and with thee will I shatter the young man and the maid; ²³and with thee will I shatter the shepherd and his flock, and with thee will I shatter the husbandman and his yoke of oxen, and with thee will I shatter governors and deputies. ²⁴And I will render unto Babylon and to all the inhabitants of Chaldea all their evil that they have done in Zion, in your sight; saith the Lord.

²⁵Behold, I am against thee, O destroying mountain, saith the Lord, which destroyest all the earth; and I will stretch out My hand upon thee, and roll thee down from the rocks, and will make thee a burnt mountain. ²⁶And they shall not take of thee a stone for a corner, nor a stone for foundations; but thou shalt be desolate for ever, saith the Lord.

²⁷Set ye up a standard in the land, blow the horn among the nations, prepare the nations against her, call together against her the kingdoms of Ararat, Minni, and Ashkenaz; appoint a marshal against her; cause the horses to come up as the rough canker-worm. ²⁸Prepare against her the nations, the kings of the Medes, the governors thereof, and all the deputies thereof, and all the land of his dominion.

²⁹And the land quaketh and is in pain; for the purposes of the Lord are performed against Babylon, to make the land of Babylon a desolation, without inhabitant.

³⁰The mighty men of Babylon have forborne to fight, they

remain in their strongholds; their might hath failed, they are become as women; her dwelling-places are set on fire; her bars are broken. ³¹One post runneth to meet another, and one messenger to meet an other, to tell the king of Babylon That his city is taken on every quarter; ³²and the fords are seized, and the castles they have burned with fire, and the men of war are affrighted.

³³For thus saith the Lord of hosts, the God of Israel: The daughter of Babylon is like a threshing-floor at the time when it is trodden; yet a little while, and the time of harvest shall come for her.

³⁴Nebuchadrezzar the king of Babylon hath devoured me, he hath crushed me, he hath set me down as an empty vessel, he hath swallowed me up like a dragon, he hath filled his maw with my delicacies; he hath washed me clean.

³⁵'The violence done to me and to my flesh be upon Babylon', shall the inhabitant of Zion say; and: 'My blood be upon the inhabitants of Chaldea', Shall Jerusalem say.

³⁶Therefore thus saith the Lord: Behold, I will plead thy cause, and take vengeance for thee; and I will dry up her sea, and make her fountain dry. ³⁷And Babylon shall become heaps, a dwelling-place for jackals, an astonishment, and a hissing, without inhabitant.

³⁸They shall roar together like young lions; they shall growl as lions' whelps. ³⁹With their poison I will prepare their feast, and I will make them drunken, that they may be convulsed, and sleep a perpetual sleep, and not wake, saith the Lord. ⁴⁰I will bring them down like lambs to the slaughter, like rams with he-goats.

⁴¹How is Sheshach taken! And the praise of the whole earth seized! How is Babylon become an astonishment among the nations!

⁴²The sea is come up upon Babylon; she is covered with the multitude of the waves thereof. ⁴³Her cities are become a desolation, A dry land, and a desert, a land wherein no man dwelleth, neither doth any son of man pass thereby.

⁴⁴And I will punish Bel in Babylon, and I will bring forth out of his mouth that which he hath swallowed up, and the nations shall not flow any more unto him; yea, the wall of Babylon shall fall.

⁴⁵My people, go ye out of the midst of her, and save

yourselves every man from the fierce anger of the Lord. [46]And let not your heart faint, neither fear ye, for the rumour that shall be heard in the land; for a rumour shall come one year, and after that in another year a rumour, and violence in the land, ruler against ruler.

[47]Therefore behold, the days come, that I will do judgment upon the graven images of Babylon, and her whole land shall be ashamed; and all her slain shall fall in the midst of her. [48]Then the heaven and the earth, and all that is therein, shall sing for joy over Babylon; for the spoilers shall come unto her from the north, saith the Lord. [49]As Babylon hath caused the slain of Israel to fall, so at Babylon shall fall the slain of all the land.

[50]Ye that have escaped the sword, Go ye, stand not still; remember the Lord from afar, and let Jerusalem come into your mind. [51]'We are ashamed, because we have heard reproach, confusion hath covered our faces; for strangers are come into the sanctuaries of the Lord's house.' [52]Wherefore, behold, the days come, saith the Lord, that I will do judgment upon her graven images; and through all her land the wounded shall groan. [53]Though Babylon should mount up to heaven, and though she should fortify the height of her strength, yet from Me shall spoilers come unto her, saith the Lord.

[54]Hark! a cry from Babylon, and great destruction from the land of the Chaldeans! [55]For the Lord spoileth Babylon, and destroyeth out of her the great voice; and their waves roar like many waters, the noise of their voice is uttered; [56]for the spoiler is come upon her, even upon Babylon, and her mighty men are taken, their bows are shattered; for the Lord is a God of recompenses, He will surely requite. [57]And I will make drunk her princes and her wise men, her governors and her deputies, and her mighty men; and they shall sleep a perpetual sleep, and not wake, saith the King, whose name is the Lord of hosts.

[58]Thus saith the Lord of hosts: The broad walls of Babylon shall be utterly overthrown, and her high gates shall be burned with fire; and the peoples shall labour for vanity, and the nations for the fire; and they shall be weary.

Read the Prophecies in Babylon (51:59-64a)

The final passage of the Book of Prophecies Against the Nations tells the story of how Jeremiah sent a messenger to Babylon to read his prophecy about its destruction.

The passage is clearly not authentic. It describes an event that supposedly happened at a time when Zedekiah had submitted to Babylon, when Jeremiah was wearing a yoke to symbolize his support for submission, and when Jeremiah was prophesying that Babylonian domination was inevitable. It is not plausible that Jeremiah prophesied destruction of Babylon at this time, and it is even less plausible that he would provoke the great power's hostility by sending the prophecy of destruction to be read in Babylon.

51:59The word which Jeremiah the prophet commanded Seraiah the son of Neriah, the son of Mahseiah, when he went with Zedekiah the king of Judah to Babylon in the fourth year of his reign. Now Seraiah was quartermaster. 60And Jeremiah wrote in one book all the evil that should come upon Babylon, even all these words that are written concerning Babylon. 61And Jeremiah said to Seraiah: 'When thou comest to Babylon, then see that thou read all these words, 62and say: O Lord, Thou hast spoken concerning this place, to cut it off, that none shall dwell therein, neither man nor beast, but that it shall be desolate for ever. 63And it shall be, when thou hast made an end of reading this book, that thou shalt bind a stone to it, and cast it into the midst of the Euphrates; 64aand thou shalt say: Thus shall Babylon sink, and shall not rise again because of the evil that I will bring upon her; and they shall be weary.'

End of Book (64b)

51:64bThus far are the words of Jeremiah.

Historical Epilog
(Chapter 52)

The historical epilog in the final chapter of the Book of Jeremiah does not mention Jeremiah. Much of it is identical to the conclusion to the history of Judah's kings in 2 Kings 24:18-25:30, but there are some differences.

In Jeremiah 52:21-23, the epilog has a more detailed description of the pillars that the Babylonians took from the temple than 2 Kings 25:17.

The epilog does not include the description of the appointment of Gedaliah as governor, his death, and the flight of Judeans to Egypt, which are in 2 Kings 25:22-26. It is odd that this is left out, since it is important to the story of Jeremiah that he was brought to Egypt by the fleeing Judeans.

The epilog includes a paragraph that is not in 2 Kings summarizing three times when Judeans were exiled to Babylonian (52:28-30), which contrasts with the story in the rest of Jeremiah and in 2 Kings and 2 Chronicles saying that there were two exiles, one at the end of the reign of Jehoiachin and one at the end of the reign of Zedekiah. This may indicate that the epilog was written by exiles in Babylon who had their own traditions about their origins.

The epilog seems to have been added, at least in part, to mitigate the story of Jehoiachin. Earlier in the book of Jeremiah, Jehoiachin was imprisoned by Nebuchadnezzar. Both 2 Kings (2 Kings 25:27-30) and this epilog say that, after he was imprisoned for thirty-seven years, the next king of Babylon, Evil-merodach, released him and treated him kindly. There is no mention of kind treatment of Zedekiah, who was blinded and imprisoned in Babylon.

52:1Zedekiah was one and twenty years old when he began to reign; and he reigned eleven years in Jerusalem; and his mother's name was Hamutal the daughter of Jeremiah of Libnah. 2And he did that which was evil in the sight of the Lord, according to all that Jehoiakim had done. 3For through the anger of the Lord did it come to pass in Jerusalem and Judah, until He had cast them out from His presence. And Zedekiah rebelled against the king of Babylon. 4And it came to pass in the ninth year of his reign, in the tenth month, in the tenth day of the month, that Nebuchadrezzar king of Babylon came, he and all his army, against Jerusalem, and encamped against it; and they built forts against it round about. 5So the city was besieged unto the eleventh year of king Zedekiah. 6In the fourth month, in the ninth day of the month, the famine was sore in the city, so that there was no bread for the people of the land. 7Then a breach was made in the city, and all the men of war fled, and went forth out of the city by night by the way of the gate between the two walls, which was by the king's garden—now the Chaldeans were against the city round about—and they went by the way of the Arabah. 8But the army of the Chaldeans pursued after the king, and overtook Zedekiah in the plains of Jericho; and all his army was scattered from him. 9Then they took the king, and carried him up unto the king of Babylon to Riblah in the land of Hamath; and he gave judgment upon him. 10And the king of Babylon slew the sons of Zedekiah before his eyes; he slew also all the princes of Judah in Riblah. 11And he put out the eyes of Zedekiah; and the king of Babylon bound him in fetters, and carried him to Babylon, and put him in prison till the day of his death.

12Now in the fifth month, in the tenth day of the month, which was the nineteenth year of king Nebuchadrezzar, king of Babylon, came Nebuzaradan the captain of the guard, who stood before the king of Babylon, into Jerusalem; 13and he burned the house of the Lord, and the king's house; and all the houses of Jerusalem, even every great man's house, burned he with fire. 14And all the army of the Chaldeans, that were with the captain of the guard, broke down all the walls of Jerusalem round about. 15Then Nebuzaradan the captain of the guard carried away captive of the poorest sort of the people, and the residue of the people that remained in the city, and those that fell away, that fell to the king of Babylon, and the residue of the multitude. [16]But Nebuzaradan the captain of the guard left of the poorest of the land to be vinedressers and husbandmen. [17]And the pillars of brass that were in the house of the Lord, and the bases and the brazen sea that were in the house of the Lord, did the Chaldeans break in pieces, and carried all the brass of them to Babylon. [18]The pots also, and the shovels, and the snuffers, and the basins, and the pans, and all the vessels of brass wherewith they ministered, took they away. [19]And the cups, and the fire-pans, and the basins, and the pots, and the candlesticks, and the pans, and the bowls—that which was of gold, in gold, and that which was of silver, in silver—the captain of the guard took away. [20]The two pillars, the one sea, and the twelve brazen bulls that were under the bases, which king Solomon had made for the house of the Lord—the brass of all these vessels was without weight. [21]And as for the pillars, the height of the one pillar was eighteen cubits; and a line of twelve cubits did compass it; and the thickness thereof was four fingers; it was hollow. [22]And a capital of brass was upon it; and the height of the one capital was five cubits, with network and pomegranates upon the capital round about, all of brass; and the second pillar also had like unto these, and pomegranates. [23]And there were ninety and six pomegranates on the outside; all the pomegranates were a hundred upon the network round about.

[24]And the captain of the guard took Seraiah the chief priest, and Zephaniah the second priest, and the three keepers of the door; [25]and out of the city he took an officer that was set over the men of war; and seven men of them that saw the king's face, who were found in the city; and the scribe of the captain of the host, who mustered the people of the land; and threescore men of the people of the land, that were found in the midst of the city. [26]And Nebuzaradan the captain of the guard took them, and brought them to the king of Babylon to Riblah. [27]And the king of Babylon smote them, and put them to death at Riblah in the land of Hamath.

So Judah was carried away captive out of his land.

[28]This is the people whom Nebuchadrezzar carried away captive: in the seventh year three thousand Jews and three and twenty; [29]in the eighteenth year of Nebuchadrezzar, from Jerusalem, eight hundred thirty and two persons; [30]in the three and twentieth year of Nebuchadrezzar Nebuzaradan the captain of the guard carried away captive of the Jews seven hundred forty and five persons; all the persons were four thousand and six hundred.

[31]And it came to pass in the seven and thirtieth year of the captivity of Jehoiachin king of Judah, in the twelfth month, in the five and twentieth day of the month, that Evil-merodach king of Babylon, in the first year of his reign, lifted up the head of Jehoiachin king of Judah, and brought him forth out of prison. [32]And he spoke kindly to him, and set his throne above the throne of the kings that were with him in Babylon. [33]And he changed his prison garments, and did eat bread before him continually all the days of his life. [34]And for his allowance, there was a continual allowance given him of the king of Babylon, every day a portion until the day of his death, all the days of his life.

Made in the USA
Coppell, TX
01 July 2023

18661272R10092